Thomas More

The King's Good Servant

Thomas More

The King's Good Servant

GORDON RUPP

COLLINS

Published by Collins
London · Glasgow
Cleveland · New York · Toronto
Sydney · Auckland · Johannesburg

Original edition
© Verlag Herder, Freiburg im Breisgau 1978

First published in Great Britain 1978
UK ISBN 0 00 211862 9

First published in the USA June/July 1978
Library of Congress Catalog Card Number 78-56261
USA ISBN 0-529-05494-9
© Gordon Rupp 1978

Photographs by Helmuth Nils Loose

Set in Monotype Garamond
Made and printed in Great Britain by
William Collins Sons & Co. Ltd, Glasgow

CONTENTS

PART ONE

'For All Seasons'—*Spring*

Thomas More was what the eighteenth century called a man of parts: citizen of renown, man of law, man of learning, man of affairs: Secretary to King Henry VIII: High Steward of both Oxford and Cambridge Universities: Speaker of the House of Commons: Lord Chancellor. Prisoner of conscience, confessor, martyr, saint. Almost all men spoke well of him in his lifetime and the admiring chorus still rightly swells. But uncritical romanticism only harms his memory, and we do him no service by ignoring his blind spots, those vulnerabilities which all men have, and which in his case do not amount to very much. But as in the case of St Francis we need to be critical of stories since as More said 'a tale that fleeth through many mouths catcheth many new feathers'. In any case there is an abundance of reliable evidence: his own writings, his correspondence and that of his contemporaries: the collections of State Papers: the ingenuous but splendid little life by his son-in-law, William Roper.

He was born 6/7 February 1477/8 in the Cripplegate ward of the City of London, and whether within or without the wall, in hearing of Bow Bells.

More was a Londoner, and he had that dead pan quality of humour which is as recognizable and distinct as that of a Brooklyn taxi driver. He loved its streets and the evocative names of its buildings, so that London almost steals the show in his chronicle of Richard III. His is the tale of one great city – not the faceless immensity we know, nor yet the 'great wen' of William Cobbett, nor yet the unsurpassed fair sight of Wordsworth's sonnet, or the rebuilt glories of Wren recaptured for us by Canaletto. More's London was a place where people lived, a community where people knew where to go to find 'one Pottier dwelling in Redcross Street' or that raddled hag, once a beauty, Elizabeth Shore, and where, fatefully, friends and enemies grew up alongside one another, like Thomas More and Richard Rich. If you walk the deserted streets of that city, on a Sunday when its mighty heart is lying still, you will see how the streets and lanes have kept their ancient names, and twists and turns, while now and then an ancient building or a scrap of garden recalls the old city More knew.

And it is a tale of a river – not the polluted reaches, the brown colour of cold tea, which we know today. But that Thames to which men put a word they also applied to Thomas More – *suavis* – sweet – a silver king's highway, the one broad continuing road, along which More continually travelled from Greenwich to Sheen and Hampton Court, with Westminster and Lambeth in between, in little cockle boats which tilted or, as Lord Chancellor in a stately barge with liveried watermen. A Thames, too, which came to his doors at Bucklersbury and Chelsea and lapped darkly against Tower Wharf and Traitors' Gate.

More's family background was affluent trade, the little world of butcher, baker and candlestick maker. His father, John More, was a lawyer, rising to moderate wealth and eminence, to become a Knight and a Judge with a country house at Gobions, North Mimms, Hertfordshire. Four times married, he covered his uxoriousness with the kind of jokes about wives which Samuel Weller, Sr in *The Pickwick Papers* reserved for widows, a trait inherited by his son.

Thomas went to St Antony's school, a grammar school which generally won a rather modern inter-schools debating competition annually staged in Smithfield. Here 'ground he at grammar' and mastered Latin. But in an age which reckoned manners and morals as large a part of education as learning, his father was happy to place his bright son in the household of the admirable John Morton, Archbishop of Canterbury and Lord Chancellor.

We have no such glimpse of Thomas waiting at table as we have of his contemporary Stephen Gardiner who as a page in Paris once prepared a buttered lettuce for the distinguished guest Erasmus. But if Roper's story be true and Thomas would

> at Christmas tide suddenly . . . step in among the players and make a part of his own . . .

(such interludes were not unknown) we may remember More's wry comment about the dangers of such impromptu goings on:

> they that sometimes step up and play . . . when they cannot play their parts, they disorder the play and do themselves no good.

The Man of Law

John More (like John Luther with regard to his son Martin) intended his son for the law, but when Morton sent Thomas to Oxford, other options seemed to open. It is a plausible guess that he may have gone to Canterbury College (later incorporated into Christchurch), but there is no certain evidence how he spent his time. However, his father abruptly recalled him to London and his vocation as a lawyer.

In that anti-clerical age, many turned from the Church as a profitable calling towards the law, and the ranks of the lawyers were thickening. But law meant more than the means of making money and reputation in the More family. His brother-in-law, his sons-in-law, were to be lawyers and some of these kinsmen, like the Ropers, were of distinguished legal families. Nor did the legal profession inhibit sound learning. At this time the Inns of Court of London were, as has often been said, a kind of third university when much of the life of Oxford and Cambridge was addled and introverted. They had their own intricate ladder of training, an ongoing and effective professional discipline embracing theory and practice. To them came a growing number of young men, from the merchant class and from the gentry, an intelligent and articulate Christian laity, such as in the next generation would make an appreciative audience in the Temple for the great debates between Richard Hooker and Walter Travers.

More made his way steadily up the rungs of the professional ladder. New Inn, Lincoln's Inn: then for three years Reader at Furnivall's Inn (1501): he was called to the Bar in 1503: then in 1510 Autumn Reader at Lincoln's Inn and Lent Reader in 1514: a member of that legal gentleman's club, Doctors' Commons, needing only his Serjeanty to put him on the inevitable road to a knighthood and the Bench.

This was his profession, his skilled mystery, where he spent most of his time and made his money. He had the gifts of a lawyer, eloquence, wit and fairness, he was no respecter of persons, and was incorruptible. He knew well how to put a case and not less fatefully, how to refrain even from good words, and to keep his own counsel. He was a success, and popular with his young men, some of whom copied his way of letting his gown slip carelessly off one shoulder, much as the young parsons of Oxford would flop down in the pulpit in imitation of Cardinal Newman in a later day.

According to William Roper, Thomas More was a member of Parliament in 1504, and successfully opposed the grant to the King of 'three fifteenths for the marriage of his eldest daughter unto the King of Scots' – 'whereupon one Mr Tiler, a gentleman of the Kings Privy Chamber, being there present, with all speed carried word to the King from the Parliament house that a beardless boy had disappointed his Grace's purpose'. We can believe in the King's annoyance, for whoso touched King Henry VII's purse, touched not trash but a main element in royal policy, though we may treat with some reserve Roper's story that the King took it out on More's father whom on some excuse he put into the Tower for debt.

The Young Humanist

Over a period of years Thomas More became increasingly involved in mercantile affairs, and in the cloth trade which was all important for London merchants. In 1509 he became Freeman of the Mercers' company and was employed in that year in intricate legal and financial negotiations on their behalf, and again in 1512 when he represented the Merchants of the Staple. He became a trusted member of delegations from the City to the King's Council, and in 1510 was made Under-Sheriff for London, also in that year representing the City in

Parliament. When the evil May Day riots broke out in London, with their ugly anti-immigrant potentiality, More took a leading part in trying to stem the violence and was prominent among those whom the frightened citizens sent to plead for mercy from the King.

But in those years, with the energy of youth and the industry of genius, he did not live by bread alone. Whatever his learned connections with Oxford, he found himself at home in London amid a group of scholars who were among the most forward looking in England. 'Humanist' is a portmanteau word, and some of the questions involved in its use need not be mentioned here.

Suffice it to say that in More's early manhood, there were groups of scholars in Universities, in cities and at the courts of kings, laymen and churchmen who shared common intellectual interests. They sought the renewal of learning and of religion, through a return to the fountain heads of Christian culture, in the revival of the classical heritage from Greece and Rome, and in going back behind the later Schoolmen to the world of the New Testament and of the first centuries. They sought to revive an old world in order to redress the balance of the new. If they looked backward, it was like a rower who looks back in order to move forward.

We err if we over-estimate the coherence of such groups, or suppose them to have had a conscious and articulate common programme for the rebirth of Christendom. There was no society of humanists of which one could be a fully paid up member, and we must not reconstruct from their writings a kind of Identikit 'humanist' to which we then make individuals conform. But if their new tools and methods were more important than their ideals, they were of great moment and while it is very difficult to gauge the role of intellectuals in any society, the Protestant and Catholic reformations of the sixteenth century would have been impossible without them, or the breakthrough into the critical learning of the modern world.

They were not primarily centred in the Universities and their institutions – such as Conrad Celtis's school of Poetry and Mathematics in Vienna, and Busleiden's college of the Sacred Languages at Louvain camped down on the fringes of the learned world. They often were in tension and conflict with the older theologians, who disdainfully regarded these academic squatters, who in turn accused the theologians of obscurantism. They themselves were perhaps not as good as they thought they were, and often on the verge of dilettantism and romanticism of a too precious kind. They were great letter writers, and their writings formed a network of correspondence across Europe, the kind of scholarly dialogue which the learned world now conducts through conferences and quarterly reviews. In their letters they buttered one another up with self-conscious Latinity (Erasmus, as P. S. Allen said used only the best butter, but others were not as tasty). But if they were a great mutual admiration society, they were prone also to gaffes and tiffs. If theologians tended to hunt in packs, and like dogs, to bark and bite, humanists were more like cats who walked by themselves and when incensed, tended to spit and scratch in hyper-sensitive controversies such as those in which Erasmus frequently engaged, and it must be said, as did More with the French poet Brixius.

But if they opened and altered or suppressed one another's letters and treated their friends' manuscripts as their own to print or not to print, there was an admirable common bond of love for mental fight. They grouped in cities – Paris, Vienna, Nuremberg – and along rivers – for there was a Society of the Vistula, of the Danube and of the Rhine. So it was in London, by the Thames. More founded such a group with William Grocyn and Thomas Linacre, and John Colet, with Cuthbert Tunstall and John Fisher near at hand. These English scholars stood within an historic English theological tradition of Platonic Augustinianism, and several of them had been to Northern Italy where they had contact with the Neo-Platonism of the Florentine Academy, with its interest in the revival of the writings of Dionysius the Areopagite, and the Hebrew mysticism of the Cabbala – a pattern of learning which spread to Reuchlin in Germany and Le Fèvre in Paris. So in England Colet and Grocyn commented and lectured on Dionysius, and this astonishing young layman, Thomas More, lectured in St Lawrence Jewry to a city audience on St Augustine's *City of God*, and took time off from his many duties to translate the life of the young Florentine genius, John Pico della Mirandola.

For the young scholar, in every part of Christendom, the way up was the same. He began by writing epigrams and poems, some in Latin and some in the vernacular, which were hopefully dedicated to eminences in Church and State: examples of this were Vadianus in Vienna, Erasmus in Holland, Melanchthon in Tübingen, More in London. He next tried his hand at translating – a bit from the classics or a short writing of the Fathers – like Tyndale in Gloucestershire, or Spalatin in Saxony, and More and Erasmus with their translations from Lucian (1505-6). Or, though this was a rather Teutonic ploy, he wrote historical narrative of a patriotic kind, after the manner of Trithemius and Wimpfeling and Spalatin in Germany, and Stumpf and Kessler in Switzerland – More's *Richard III* is an example of this. Not that these men were only interested in letters. In this first age of printing they delighted in the very feel of a book and the quality of its print, and began to collect their own libraries. They were interested in natural history, astronomy and the new lands beyond the sea. There are many resemblances between Thomas More and Conrad Peutinger, the Recorder of Augsburg and a lay humanist, who kept a parrot as More kept an ape, to remind him of the New World, and whose collection of books, coins and maps was famous: who went like More on embassies (they once met at Bruges): who like More severely examined heretics and who above all was surrounded by a bevy of educated women – Margaret, his wife, took on Erasmus at Greek and Constance, like Meg Roper, wrote witty Latin letters to her father.

Of More's inner life we know but little. There are some enigmatic phrases in a letter to Colet (1504) lamenting his absence from London:

> By following your footsteps I had escaped almost from the very gates of hell and now driven by some force and necessity, I am falling back again into gruesome darkness. I am like Eurydice except that she was lost because Orpheus looked back at her, but I am sinking because you do not look back at me.

It would not be like even the young More to round off a really deep spiritual crisis with a classical allusion, and it certainly cannot be used as evidence that More at this time was troubled by sceptical 'doubts' (a nineteenth- and twentieth-century disease).

But Erasmus and Roper plausibly report that More had seriously considered entering the priesthood and even joining a religious order, and that alongside his legal studies 'he gave himself wholly to devotion and prayer in the Charterhouse at London, living there religiously'.

Certainly he always kept up links with the Carthusians, the order which, never having been deformed, as was said, needed no reformation, and whose strict discipline was itself a warning to the half-hearted. But it was an age of growing aversion from the older forms and with a new emphasis on lay spirituality and while throughout More's life there was never absent a deep undertow, bearing him towards a life of ascetic contemplation, once he had made his decision he committed himself entirely to the life of a devout layman in the world.

I am inclined to take seriously the comment of Erasmus that 'when his blood was warm, he did not flee the love of women but conducted himself with honour' and the further comment that 'he nearly took orders, but the attractions of marriage proved so strong that he determined to be a chaste husband rather than a lewd Priest' – in his last prayers in the Tower the phrase 'Remember not the sins of my youth' is underlined. We do not know when More first took to wearing a hair shirt, but it was certainly not for ornamental purposes, but for the taming of the flesh and as a work of penitence.

The time came when his attendance at the Charterhouse gave way to visits to the home of Sir John Colt MP, a neighbour of his father's at Gobions, and though attracted by one daughter, like the miner 'forty-niner', in 1505 he married her sister for unromantic reasons. Jane Colt faithfully bore him a child a year – Margaret, Elizabeth, Cicely, John and in between put up with her older husband's well meaning attempts to train her in music and letters. There is something of a mystery about More's second marriage. Erasmus's explanation that the children had to be looked after (Thomas Cromwell, similarly bereft with a small brood, never re-married) does not explain its swiftness, as reported by More's parish priest:

> I buried his first wife, and within a month after, he came to me on a Saturday night late and there brought me a dispensation to be married the next Monday without any banns asking.

To marry a second time meant putting ideas of the priesthood, if they still existed, right away and the lady was his senior by some years, a widow with a family.

But if Alice Middleton was no chicken, nor no beauty, she could keep her end up in forthright talk, and the teasing banter between them is strangely like that between Luther and his Kate. Like Kate Luther she could handle his affairs as was shown when, during More's absence in 1529 there was a disastrous fire in More's house when barns were destroyed in which More had allowed neighbours to store corn:

> I pray you to make some good search what my poor neighbours have lost and bid them take no thought therefore, for and I should not leave myself a spoon there shall no poor neighbour of mine bear no loss by any chance happened in my house . . . devise somewhat with your friends what way were best to take provision to be made for corn for our household and for seed this year coming.

She did not take kindly to his foreign guests and Ammonius and Erasmus with their interminable Latin conversations, their 'in' jokes and their finicky eating habits, evidently got on her nerves.

More's 'merry tales' are not to be mealy-mouthed about, but taken with some of his imagery and things like his obsessive references to Luther's marriage, seem to add up to something and it is no discredit to More if we surmise that he was in the words of the song 'a rather susceptible Chancellor'.

This, then, was Thomas More in his spring time, a coming man, of rising reputation in the City and at the Bar, a cherished member of an international company of scholars, with his young children round him and for whom many doors were opening. His narrative, written in these years, of the reign of Richard III, is a not untypical historical piece, never printed in his life, but existing in Latin and English versions. It was incorporated into the chronicles of Grafton and Hall, and thence into Shakespeare's (and Laurence Olivier's) picture of Richard III as a croaking tyrant, the entirely evil hunchback of Crosby Square. It is a view contested by many writers and though to this day the inhabitants of the Yorkshire village of Sheriff Hutton, where the ruins of one of his castles stands, have kept down the centuries a belief in his goodness, perhaps More's reading is the plausible one. No doubt it is meant as a cautionary tale, though it draws no overt moral. It is full of satire and has some fine comic touches, and there is the famous compassionate picture of Edward IV's concubine, Elizabeth Shore, that fifteenth-century Lady Hamilton, no better than she might have been, but a good sight better than the hypocrites who condemned her:

> I doubt not some shall think this woman too slight a thing to be written of and set among the remembrance of great matters: which they shall specially think who happily shall esteem her only by what they now see her. But me seemeth the chance so much the more worthy to be remembered, in how much she is now in the more beggarly condition, unfriended and worn out of acquaintance, after as great favour with the prince, after as great suit and seeking to with all those that those days had business to speed, as many other men were in those times, which be now famous only by the infamy of their ill deeds. Her doings were not much less, albeit they be much less remembered, because they were not so evil . . . for at this day she beggeth of many at this day living, that at this day had begged if she had not been.

When we have discussed More's sources, and classical models, in Livy and Tacitus and More's memories of conversations with Archbishop Morton, we come back with the frequent 'Many say . . . some say . . .' to the citizens of London, the whispering gallery of common report, which More as a lawyer did not despise. There are flashbacks to the chaos of the Wars of the Roses and the evil of a 'diversity of titles' to the throne which implicitly underlines the virtues of the house of Tudor.

Erasmus

When Thomas More first met the celebrated man of letters Desiderius Erasmus, the Dutchman was simply an interesting young scholar on the look out for money, patronage and some place of learning. Not until the publication of his proverbs (*Adagia*, 1503) and his edifying tract the *Enchiridion*, (1504) did he begin to attract notice and fame, which grew rapidly until his *Praise of Folly*

(1509), and his editions of the New Testament (1516) and of the Fathers made him pre-eminent among the scholars north of the Alps. By this time he had come to be at the centre of a vast spider's web of correspondence. He is one of the very great letter writers and like all the others, an inveterate gossip. But his friendship with More was something special.

In 1499 More took his friend for a stroll which ended at Eltham Palace, where he introduced him to the royal children and a solemn little Prince Henry quizzed his visitor in Latin, while Erasmus hid his chagrin that he had come out without a complimentary poem up his sleeve. Erasmus never quite got over the shock, as far as England was concerned, of having his literary winnings confiscated by the Customs men at Dover, and More kept an eye on his financial affairs thereafter, involving himself in a series of borderline wangles on the edge of legality, and did what he could to extend the area of patronage which perhaps overall disappointed Erasmus.

Although Erasmus's pen portrait of his friend, as he described him to Ulrich von Hutten, is celebrated like most of his eulogies, it has to be taken with a pinch of salt.

> More is neither tall or short in build or stature . . . he is light complexioned . . . neither sallow nor ruddy . . . his hair is auburn touching upon the black . . . his eyes are of a blue grey colour . . . his face is a mirror of his nature reflecting his kindness and a hearty friendliness that holds a hint of ready banter . . . a face more suggestive of gaiety than dignity or serious gravity. His right shoulder appears slightly more elevated than his left, and this trait, most readily apparent in his walk, is not congenital but . . . a product of habit.

Erasmus adds that More cared little for fine clothes or delicate food:

> It is his habit to prefer beef, salt meat and common fermented bread to the usual delicacies – he has a special liking for milk pudding and takes great relish in a bowl of eggs.

There are personal glimpses from other sources. William Roper, who must at times have been an irritating son-in-law, says that in twenty years he never saw More in a fume. Some humanists cultivated an artificial *bonhomie*, and grinned like dogs when they ran about their cities. But there was nothing affected about More's affability and kindness. No account of More could omit Robert Whittinton's tribute to him (1520):

> More is a man of angel's wit and singular learning. I know not his fellow. For where is the man of that gentleness, lowliness and affability? And as time requireth, a man of marvellous mirth and pastimes and sometime of a sad gravity. A man for all seasons.

Edward Hall complained that More never made a speech without taking the rise out of somebody or something. And More for whom little jokes were the small coin of daily life, but who could write satires on the grand scale was the kind of man who annoys sadly those without a sense of humour. But with More we need to remember what G. K. Chesterton taught us all over again, that when a humorist makes a joke he is not simply 'trying to be funny', but often uses humour to make his most serious points. And of such, if the parables of Jesus are anything to go by, is the Kingdom of Heaven.

It was this common trait which made Erasmus and More agreeably collaborate in a translation of the classical satirist, Lucian. Satire may be a powerful instrument of social criticism and as such, the tool of reform, and the humanists used it to attack obscurantism and superstition, and what Burnet called the 'superannuated Judaism' of much contemporary religion. In those years there were some notable satires, the *Letters of Obscure Men*, the *Julius Exclusus* and Erasmus's *Praise of Folly*, written in More's house.

More at this time was much occupied in journeyings. In October 1515 he was sent on a diplomatic mission to the Low Countries which was led by Cuthbert Tunstall. In the course of it he met Erasmus, and the wealthy layman Busleiden. But his great discovery in friendship was Peter Gilles, the Chief Secretary of Antwerp, and one of those, who like Lazarus Spengler in Nuremberg, Conrad Peutinger in Augsburg and Stefan Roth in Zwickau, combined civil service with a love of letters. There were two by-products of this meeting. One was the beautiful diptych which Erasmus and Gilles commissioned Quentin Metsys to paint, in which the two men face one another across a table – which they sent as a gift to More (who paid? – probably Gilles). The other was More's *Utopia*.

Utopia

The work for which More is best remembered began as a kind of counterpoint to Erasmus's *Praise of Folly*, as an intellectual lark. More seems to have had no thought, as had the young John Milton, of writing something mankind would not willingly let die. But this he did. One of the great things about it is the relaxed and happy way he wrote it, so different from the earnest rabbinism of commentators who have read so much into and out of its pages. But perhaps fresh readers need to be reminded that it is a great work of the imagination, to be read first of all for delight, as a work which has more in common with the *Ancient Mariner* or *Alice in Wonderland* than with Marx's *Das Kapital*.

It has been observed how often literature centres on the theme of a group of

Spring

The Island of Utopia. A woodcut by Ambrosius Holbein, which was in the 1518 Basel edition of More's best known work. It shows Raphael Hythlodaeus (left) pointing out the island with its town of Amaurotum (City of Dreams) at the top centre. THE TRUSTEES OF THE BRITISH MUSEUM, LONDON.

19

friends, talking in a garden. Not only Plato's *Republic* but the Bible begin in that way. *Utopia*, or *Nusquama – Nowhere*, or *The Never Never Land*, begins with a mossy seat in the garden of Peter Gilles's house where he and More, and More's young 'famulus' John Clement, listen to a stranger, Raphael Hythlodaye as he tells what he has seen in foreign lands, after being left behind on one of the recently famed voyages of Amerigo Vespucci.

More's age was as fascinated by these voyages to the edge of the world as ours is by outer space, and indeed *Utopia* has some striking similarities with science fiction. It is significant that Hythlodaye is Portuguese, for it was Portugal which had the edge, even of Spain in such exploration, and for half a century Portuguese sailors and traders had been bringing back tales from East and West and South and North, about new and ancient lands, and islands full of marvels.

More's *Utopia* has so much in common with contemporary travellers' tales that we can almost believe that the Vicar of Croydon was serious when he offered to go as missionary Bishop to Utopia.

Here is a description by an English merchant of the rich island of Ormuz:

Ormuz is an island in circuit about 25 or 30 miles and is the driest island in the world: for there is nothing growing in it but salt: for their water, wood or victuals and all things necessary come out of Persia which is about twelve miles from thence.

Yet this island produced the finest pearls, the author says, in the world. It is not more or less probable than the marvels of Utopia:

The island of Utopia extends in the centre where it is broadest for two hundred miles and is not much narrower for the after part of the island, but towards both ends it begins gradually to taper. Those ends form a circle five hundred miles in circumference and so make the island look like a new moon, the horns of which are divided by straits about eleven miles across. . . . .

The island contains fifty-four city states all spacious and magnificent, identical in language, traditions, customs and laws. They are similar also in layout and everywhere, as far as the nature of the ground permits, similar even in appearance. None of them is separated by less than twenty-four miles from the nearest, but none is so isolated that a person cannot go from it to another in a day's journey on foot. From each city three old and experienced citizens meet to discuss the affairs of common interest to the island once a year at Amaurotum, for this city, being in the very centre of the country is situated most conveniently for the representatives of all sections.

The Anydrus rises eighty miles above Amaurotum from a spring not very large: but being increased by several tributaries, two of which are of fair size it is half a mile broad in front of the city. After soon becoming still broader and after running farther for sixty miles, it falls into the ocean. Through the whole distance between the city and the sea and even above the city for some miles, the tide alternately flows in for six whole hours and then ebbs with an equally speedy current. When the sea comes in, it fills the whole bed of the Anydrus with its water for a distance of thirty miles, driving the river back.

It is these apparently factual corroborative details which give verisimilitude to More's narrative.

More wrote the Introduction, with its mixture of real and fictitious persons, and then the Second part, writing the First part after he had returned to England. Into it went much of his own learning. Plato, of course, and a good deal of Augustine's *City of God* and thoughts of the Fathers about the consequences of the Fall on slavery and private property: Stoicism and that Epicureanism which had been a feature of Erasmus's *Enchiridion*. It is a great rag bag of ideas from which the most divers types may take their pick. Perhaps it is not so much its communism and sharing of property and wealth which sounds so radical as the attack on a society founded on profit and greed:

When I consider and turn over in my mind the state of all commonwealths flourishing anywhere today, so help me God, I see nothing else than a kind of conspiracy of the rich who are aiming at their own interests under the name and title of commonwealth. They invent and devise all ways and means by which they first may keep, without fear of loss, all that they have amassed by evil practices and secondly they then purchase as cheaply as possible and abuse the toil and labour of the poor. These devices become law as soon as the rich have once decreed their observance in the name of the public – that is of the poor also!

In places it resembles not so much a Soviet republic as the organized amenities of a holiday camp. It has its startlingly modern touches: incubators, terminal clinics, euthanasia, a modern attitude to crime and punishment. But is also an elitist society, there are the slaves and some grim prohibitions – of political dissent, of restricted travel, and some underlying views of the nature of society which gives point to those who see it as a fundamentally conservative document. It is, most scholars now agree, a picture of a society living under natural law, and in the light of reason, and hence its formidable challenge to a supposedly Christian society.

And in its tolerance, and a certain eclecticism there is surely a reminiscence of the fifteenth-century writings of Nicholas of Cusa and Pico della Mirandola and their search for one ultimate, reconciling human religion. Recent writers have pointed out the fundamental importance for it of community, the *familia* of the bishop's household in the time of Augustine, the *koinonia* of monastic societies, the image of that paternalistic household, the building not made with hands which More would place within the outer walls of Bucklersbury and Chelsea. The first part of More's deeply compassionate First part, shows his mental fight for England's green and pleasant land – the agricultural revolution – the decay of husbandry (where 'sheep eat up men') and of towns, the sturdy beggars, and his solutions are contemporary and simplistic. But the dominant feature of the First part is the great argument between Hythlodaye and More about the place of a philosopher in political society and when Hythlodaye affirms 'there is no place for philosophers among Kings' More replies – and it may reflect a personal decision already made:

> You do not, simply because you are unable to uproot mistaken opinions and correct long established ills, abandon the state altogether. In a storm you do not desert the ship because you are unable to control the winds . . . you must try to use subtle and indirect means . . . and what you cannot turn to good, you must make as little evil as possible.

Certainly there is political realism in More's shrewd comments on contemporary diplomacy and power struggles, and on the folly of war. More was as opposed to war on principle as his friend Erasmus, but he was perhaps more solidly 'earthed' than his friend and like his merchant friends knew what war did to trade, and like his Londoners knew about the crippling taxes, and like a Christian knew what it meant for families when destitute and crippled soldiers at last came home from the wars.

Politics is about power, but in the sixteenth century it was also about glory. Henry VIII cherished immortal longings to be another Edward III or Henry V and justify the quarterings on the arms of England of the lilies of France. His adviser Thomas Wolsey believed there was no future for neutrality for England, which in any case Henry VIII limbering up on the touchline in a great balloon of armour, would not have brooked.

'Kings' Games'

'These matters be Kings' games' More had written in his *Richard III*, 'as it were stage plays, and for the most part played upon scaffolds. In which poor men be but the lookers on. And they that be wise will meddle no further. For they that some time step up and play with them, when they cannot play their parts, they disorder the play and do themselves no good.'

It was to be true with regard to Wolsey, as he drew England more and more within that three-dimensional game between Pope, Emperor and the King of France. 'Very glorious was he', said More of Wolsey, 'and that far above measure'. But perhaps the Cardinal knew that pomp, circumstance and panache were indispensable in Renaissance diplomacy. More went on one mission after another, his skills in law, finance and his fluency in the French tongue making him a useful member of any delegation. He was in the Low Countries in 1516: at Calais for several months in 1517, and was a signer of the Peace with France in October 1518. In 1520 he attended the King to the spectacular 'Field of the Cloth of Gold' (in *Utopia* he had already condemned such costly and glittering demonstrations), and he more than once made an official oration before the Emperor Charles V. He again accompanied Wolsey to France in 1525 and 1527. But he signed for peace and in his own obituary it is only the Peace of Cambrai which he mentioned. He now had little leisure but in 1519 became involved in a silly controversy with another friend of Erasmus, the poet Brixius.

PART TWO

'For All Seasons'—*Summer*

In a naval encounter in 1512 two warships, one French, the other English, had become entangled, set on fire, blew up and sank. This was no great advertisement for either navy, but Brixius wrote patriotic epigrams and More privately replied with some unpublished verses which Erasmus stupidly published without More's permission, and which drew from Brixius a fiery *Antimorus*. There was a comic interchange of letters between More and Erasmus, in which Erasmus implored More to turn a blind eye, while More replied by suggesting Erasmus should cool it, in his own waspish encounters with Edward Lee. It is perhaps not all loss that More was torn from humanist learning and his next writing, never published, was a throwback into fifteenth-century spirituality, a discussion of the Four Last Things in which 'Merry Tales' are intermingled with sombre hell fire preaching.

The date on which More decided, with prompting from the King, to become a King's servant cannot be pin-pointed, but he was sworn into the Council before August 1517.

This was for More a solemn occasion, and before it he made his confession and heard Mass. Despite Erasmus, the golden S-Collar, with its pendent Tudor Rose, which he wears in his most famous portrait, had meaning and value for him. In his new offices, he did not lack legal business, for he took part in the tribunal which accompanied the court and which was to become the Court of Requests. In the great Eltham ordinance of 1526 More was among four who should always accompany the King. No doubt the King chose him because he liked and respected him, for his character and intelligence and wit, though it may be that More did grow a little weary of being expected to be witty, as a kind of Lord High Jester, but he obviously also loved his master, who when he wished could be a charmer. But he could not fail to note an imperious will, an appetite for power. And when at Chelsea the King

walked in Sir Thomas More's garden by the space of an hour and held his arm about Sir Thomas More's neck.

More checked Roper's admiration with the comment

I think he doth as singularly favour me as any subject within this realm. Howbeit Son Roper I may tell thee, I have no great cause to be proud thereof. But if my head could win his Majesty a castle in France – it should not fail to go.

More was unto Henry as a pleasant voice, perhaps the only one he could bear to hear after dinner, and sometimes late at night, read and interpret the diplomatic despatches from Wolsey. And sometimes when the day's hubbub would be over they would go upon the roof, and the wise man would point to the stars and explain the marvels of the heavens. In 1521 More was knighted and made Under-Treasurer of England with the salary of £173.6.8d – not an onerous post, but tied to other administrative duties which made it appropriate for Tunstall to dedicate to More an arithmetic book. It was because of his trusted relation between Cardinal and King that he was made Speaker of the House of Commons (the fee was £100 a session, but the amount was doubled at Wolsey's request). More began with a notable plea for free speech which some have seen as a landmark in the growth of parliamentary liberties. No doubt all these offices and their arduous labour come far short of the office of a philosopher at the court of Utopia but there is no reason to suppose that More harboured such high ambition. He would not have thought he had in any way failed because he did not influence high policy or revolutionize administration, any more than he failed as a lawyer because no cases or precedents were associated with his name. Unlike Stephen Gardiner and Thomas Cromwell, he did not feel the attraction of power, and had no mind to imitate the vaulting ambition of the Cardinal of England. He would be a 'King's servant' in the manner of many in that age – a Chancellor Brück in Germany, a John Cheke or William Cecil in the next decade.

'Defender of the Faith'

At the end of 1517 there appeared on the north-eastern horizon of Christendom a cloud the size of a man's fist – Martin Luther. Rapidly the whole sky darkened, though the impact of revolution was not perhaps felt in England until 1520 when Luther published his *Babylonish Captivity*, written in Latin for a learned audience, which denied at least four of the seven sacraments and attacked a whole edifice of ecclesiastical practice. Henry VIII now entered the fray in a work sufficiently his own – give and take a few arguments, quotations, and indices – for him to claim authorship. More must have been consulted, but he does not seem to have been part of the editorial team.

It was a great success for Henry VIII, and won from the Pope the compliment of a Golden Rose, and the title 'Defender of the Faith'. It did not silence Martin Luther who wrote a reply, and who, having called the Pope Anti-Christ was not going to be choosily deferential to an English King. A far more learned attack on Luther came from John Fisher, Bishop of Rochester and Chancellor of Cambridge, though later Fisher wondered if he could not have better spent his energy in prayer. There was in 1523 an anonymous reply to Luther of out-matching scurrility, under the name of 'William Rosseus', in which More certainly had a great hand, though I suspect that the part of it attributed to a

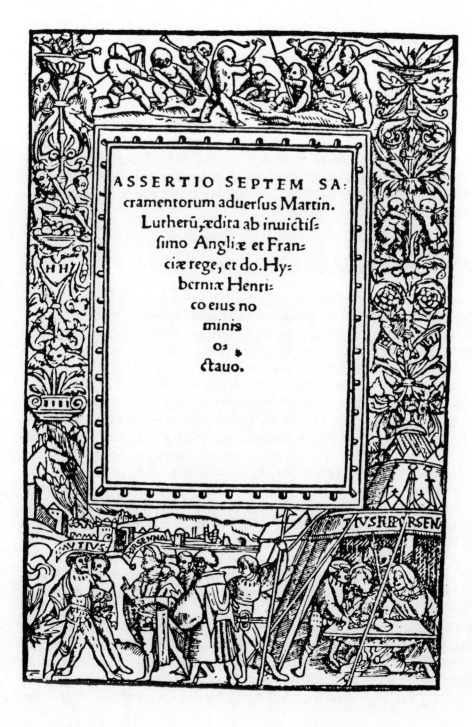

The title page of the
letter *Assertio Septum
Sacramentorum* denounc-
ing Martin Luther, which
first appeared in London
in 1521.

Spaniard, Barvellus, was actually the work of the Franciscan Thomas Murner. He had at this time come to England under a rebuke from the Council of Strasbourg for his violence of the tongue, was according to More turning his German anti-Luther tracts into Latin in this country, and was soon to leave with a royal gift of £100 which was more than anybody ever gave Erasmus in England and equalled More's stipend as Speaker. At any rate the three treatises of the King, Fisher and 'Rosseus' put England on the theological map, and other Continental anti-Lutherian writers, Eck and John Faber among them, turned aside to see this great sight. But it is of great moment that these three, Henry VIII, More and Fisher were in this apologetic field as one team and with a common mind.

The Household of Sir Thomas More

Such were the employments of Thomas More in his middle years. They had brought him eminence and affluence, though nothing like what an ambitious or avaricious politician might have gained. But he could afford to leave the rambling old house at Bucklersbury for a fine house running down to the river at Chelsea, with a sizeable garden, and where he was able to build a library, a chapel and a gallery. Here he set up his growing household, his children and their families and supervised their education while he ordered the segregated existence of the servants male and female with kindness but firm control.

With four children and eleven grandchildren, and his adopted children and wards, he formed that endearing company immortalized in the sketches and paintings of Hans Holbein. There they sit, the children, More and his wife and old Sir John, with the family jester, in a great stillness of affection, as though listening to music, as they might well have been, for they were devoted musicians and the house was continually filled with sweet sounds which gave delight and hurt not.

There is the good story of how the Duke of Norfolk visited them and was astounded to see More singing in the parish choir, clad in a surplice. The Duke, a stuffy old diehard, could not refrain from blustering 'God's Body, my Lord Chancellor, a parish clerk?'

Their life together was surrounded with devotion and began with the Penitential Psalms and Litany, a usage which made it natural for More and Margaret in the Tower of London to say those prayers before any conversation. There were other psalms at night, and during meals John More or his adopted daughter Margaret Gigs would intone scripture. And devotion and practical charity went hand in hand. Margaret Gigs would tend the sick and Margaret Roper, beside washing her father's hair shirt had care of an almshouse her father kept in Chelsea.

The higher education of women was, so to speak, 'in the air' at this time. We have seen that the Peutinger ladies in Augsburg were at the same time that More's daughters were growing up, turning into formidable bluestockings. The households of Sir Antony Cooke with his five learned daughters and the six daughters of Bishop Barlow, show that this was to be a continuing pattern, while the Princess Mary could translate Erasmus's paraphrases on St John, the Lady Jane Grey could discuss not only Greek but Hebrew, with the Zurich reformer Bullinger, and the greatest schoolmaster of the age, Roger Ascham, doted on the learned skills of his pupil, the Princess Elizabeth.

This does not mean that More was not a pioneer: 'Erudition in women' he wrote, 'is a new thing and a reproach to the sloth of man.' He carefully chose a succession of tutors, beginning with John Clement and ending with the German astronomer Nicholas Kratzer. But he was innocently proud of his daughters, especially when they were able to debate philosophy in front of the King, and he showed off their linguistic skills to his learned friends, while when he was travelling overseas he conducted a little correspondence course in Latin. Margaret Roper had little to fear from any competition even with her royal contemporaries in learning.

The end of September 1526 was memorable for the family, for on the 29th his daughters were married to William Dauncey and Giles Heron, good matches in every way, while on the following day More exchanged his office as Under-Treasurer for the more lucrative and important office of Chancellor of the Duchy of Lancaster, which called on his services as an equity judge. In 1527 his lands and fees were assessed at £340 a year.

Such was More's happy home and his eminence and prosperity when two-thirds of his life had passed. It is a moving picture of a wise judge, his family surrounding him. There is a picture too in the Old Testament of such a good, wise man and his family, blissfully unaware that they are perched on the edge of suffering and disaster. But at this time there was nothing to make More turn to that story, with its ominous and devastating line – 'Hast thou considered my servant Job?'

PART THREE

'For All Seasons'—*Autumn*

Thomas More

This eighteenth-century engraving taken from a contemporary miniature depicts Thomas More as Speaker (bottom of picture) at the opening of the English Parliament. On the right of Henry VIII (top of picture) sits Cardinal Wolsey. ROYAL LIBRARY, WINDSOR.

The Royal Divorce

We are only concerned with the 'divorce' of Henry VIII from Catherine of Aragon insofar as it affected the life and death of Thomas More. Legally, it was an intricate affair of what the prayer book calls 'lawful impediments', practically of labyrinthine diplomatic and political negotiations.

When Prince Arthur of England (aged fifteen) married Catherine of Aragon (aged sixteen) it was part of a negotiated peace between England and Spain, and when Arthur died it was decided for reasons of policy that she should marry his younger brother Henry (aged eleven). A papal dispensation was needed for a marriage well within prohibited degrees, and a bull was forthcoming from Pope Julius II. The young Henry was instructed to enter some formal protest at what had gone over his young head. But these things were long forgotten and had the marriage produced a boy, all might have been well. But as the years passed, several babies died and there were miscarriages, save for the birth of a daughter, Mary.

We must believe that Henry had serious anxiety about the succession to the throne. He was but the second in the new Tudor dynasty, with, behind them, the memory of the near anarchy of the Wars of the Roses. A daughter represented a monstrous regiment of women which Henry could not view with equanimity. His marital misfortunes began to trouble Henry's conscience, though whether they would have done so had he not fallen in love with the Lady Anne Boleyn is another matter.

It may be that a formal question from the French Bishop of Tarbes, about those earlier dispensations, set things off. Henry turned to the prohibition in Leviticus 18 against such a marriage as his and saw in those verses a prediction of the calamities which had come to pass. On the other hand as he was soon to learn there was a passage in Deuteronomy 26 which appeared to contradict this. There was in any case the question how far these commands were binding on Christian men.

The theological and biblical dilemma led on to more complicated questions. Was this prohibition of divine and moral law? – in which case it was urged, no papal dispensation could be valid. More's first off the cuff reaction was shrewd. When the King 'walking in the gallery, brake with me of his great matter' More replied that 'the greater hope of the matter stood in certain faults that were found in the bull, whereby the bull should by the law not be sufficient'. There in fact, the investigation centred and soon there were intricate wrangles between the lawyers, whether the dispensation touched only the impediment of 'affinity' and assumed that the marriage had been consummated, or whether it failed to touch a further impediment of 'public honesty'. It soon became a highly technical question far too complex for ordinary people who came to the simplistic conclusion of the play *Henry VIII*:

It seems the marriage with his brother's wife
Has crept too near his conscience.
No, his conscience
Has crept too near another lady.

Unknown to Catherine, Henry caused an action to be brought against himself by Wolsey and Warham charging him with living in sin. So complex were the issues opened up that the case had to be adjourned, and a learned commission appointed. Any hope that the matter might be quietly settled was upset by the Queen.

She had some very good advice, notably from Bishop Fisher. He early came to the conclusion that the Levitical prohibition was not binding, and that the marriage was lawful. He continued to speak and write against the divorce with an obstinacy and courage which enraged the King. But it was Catherine herself who again and again threw the opposition into disarray. She swore on the gospels and before the sacrament that her marriage with Arthur was never consummated, and this raised new legal issues. Then she revealed that there had been a second brief from Pope Julius II in which the terms of the case had been altered, a document which Henry told his emissaries to get hold of at all costs, which they failed to do. She was not moved by sinister threats, and refused to enter a nunnery. She appealed to the Pope.

Charles V was her nephew, and his feats of arms, when he encircled Pope Clement VII in the Castle of St Angelo (1527) and defeated François I at Landriane in 1529 made his the superior political pressure. But the Pope did eventually commission a legatine trial, which opened at Blackfriars under the joint presidency of Wolsey and the Cardinal Campeggio, an experienced diplomat as well as a martyr to gout which tended to upset him at convenient and inconvenient moments.

Catherine made a poignant appeal to the King, which moved the crowd, but not her husband, and Fisher made a sensational speech. But while Wolsey was in France, and on a day when the King and his advisers thronged the hall to hear the verdict, Campeggio adjourned the trial for the harvest season. It was a fatal delay, and in the light of Catherine's appeal the case was advoked to Rome, where nobody was inclined to hurry the case which dragged on for years.

The Fall of Wolsey

The immediate consequence was the fall of Wolsey. His bungling of the divorce was the excuse and perhaps the reason for dismissing a very convenient scapegoat for all the extravagances and impositions of the French Wars. The butcher's son had not come to such unparalleled eminence without making many enemies on the way, included among them Anne Boleyn. Though his learning, humanity and indeed devotion, have been under-estimated, his flamboyance and ambition were a byword. In vain did this unjust steward try to make friends with the mammon of unrighteousness by surrendering his palaces at Hampton Court and York Place (now named Whitehall). He had accumulated the highest offices in Church and State and as Cardinal Legate and as Lord Chancellor was the Pooh Bah of England.

He was entirely vulnerable when the King drew a rather rusty sword (recently evoked in 'Hunne's' case), the statutes of Praemunire which brought rather vague sanctions to bear on the intrusion of foreign jurisdiction, and Wolsey's fall, in this regard, opened the way for the subsequent humiliation of the whole spiritual estate. When Wolsey surrendered the Great Seal, Henry turned to Sir Thomas More for his new Chancellor.

It was dangerously late in the day, and More must have known that it exposed him to dangers. But he took the risk, perhaps knowing the delight that it must bring to his ancient and ailing father. Besides, the King had promised to leave him alone. The King had seen to it that More talked with his own theologians and lawyers and not only had More read deeply in the biblical and patristic authorities, but he had made known his own views, which he never put in writing, plainly to the King. Now the King renewed his goodwill:

His highness made me . . . his Chancellor of this Realm, soon after which time his grace moved me again . . . to look and consider his great matter . . . and if it were so that thereupon it should hap me to see such things as should persuade me to that part, he would gladly use me among other of his counsellors in that matter and nevertheless he graciously declared to me that he would in no wise that I should other thing do or say therein than upon that I should perceive mine own conscience to serve me, and that I should first look unto God, and after God unto him, which most gracious words was the first lesson also that ever his grace gave me at my first coming into his noble service.

Lord Chancellor

More took his oath as Chancellor on 26 October 1529. During his short spell in office he attended conscientiously to his legal and administrative duties, as ever, incorruptibly and with despatch. He left no mark on the history of the law unless it was to soften the tensions which had arisen by the frequent interventions of equity, by means of 'Injunctions' into the common law.

The King kept his word, and More on his side kept out of all discussions about the divorce, and had stopped even reading or talking about it. He must have become increasingly isolated from those at court, and have marked the new authority given to Wolsey's younger men, Stephen Gardiner and Thomas Cromwell. No doubt a good deal of frustration was worked off when he threw himself with all his energy into that old cause which had bound him and still bound him in alliance with his prince, the fight against heretical pravity.

By 1528 the situation with regard to heresy was very different from 1521 and Henry's blast of the trumpet against the monstrous arguments of Luther. More did not easily panic, but even he now spoke of heresy 'spreading like wildfire'. There was a formidable ferment among the younger scholars in the Universities and among the merchants in the cities. It had come near More's own household in the temporary defection of William Roper, in the serving boy Dick Purser who had been indoctrinated by the heretic George Joye, and in his brother-in-law John Rastell, who in trying to talk John Frith out of denying purgatory was himself converted by him. There was not any longer a question of finding and burning the learned Latin works of the Continental Reformers who included not only the Wittenberg theologians, but Zwingli, Oecolampadius, Bucer, Capito and Lambert, but a growing literature in English, and most dangerous of all, the New Testament in William Tyndale's translation (1526). More wrote to Erasmus:

> our own fellow countrymen, with a steady stream of books written in our own vernacular and containing mistranslations and worse, misinterpretations of scripture have been sending into our land every brand of heresy from Belgium.

Wolsey's government had spies and agents abroad trying to track down the damned, elusive heretics, to entice them back to England, or to denounce them to the Imperial authorities. They organized swoops on theological cannabis, and tried to trace the dumps of religious explosive. Such was the descent of More and his helpers on the Steelyard, the London house of the German Hanseatic merchants, where they found a cache of contraband literature, as a result of which several merchants were heavily fined. For the second time there was a public burning of barrels of books, at Paul's Cross, with a sermon by John Fisher. By October, large numbers of Tyndale's New Testament were entering the country and on the 24th of October Tunstall preached against it, claiming to have detected above two thousand errors (eighty-four out of every hundred words were to be incorporated in the Authorized Version of the English Bible). More himself wrote a long Open Letter against Bugenhagen, the number Three of the Wittenberg team, who had a little prematurely congratulated the English nation on its re-discovery of the gospel. It was in these circumstances that Tunstall asked More's help, to show the people 'the craft and malice of the heretics and render such folks better equipped against such impious supplanters of the Church'. More realized it was a formidable task:

> Of these books of heresies there be so many made within these few years, what by Luther himself and by his fellows, and afterward by the new sects sprung out of his . . . that the bare names of these books were almost enough to make a book, and of every sort of those books be some brought into this realm and kept in hugger mugger by some shrewd masters that keep them for no good.

The Battle of the Books

More's aim, he told Erasmus, was not the hope of convincing the heretics, but to

> protect those men who do not deliberately desert the truth, but are seduced by the enticements of clever fellows

for, as he further wrote:

> I find that breed of men absolutely loathsome, so much so that unless they regain their senses, I want to be as hateful to them as anyone can possibly be.

The first fruit of his study was the publication in June 1529 of

> A Dialogue of Sir Thomas More, Knight . . . wherein be treated divers matters as the veneration and worship of images and relics, praying to saints and going on pilgrimages . . . with many other things touching the pestilent sect of Luther and Tyndale by the one begun in Saxony and by the other laboured to be brought to England.

It is a significant title. For the first four points were those which marked off the Lollards from their orthodox neighbours, and what was happening at this time was the conjunction of old heresy with the new doctrines from the Continent.

What is the place within the Christian religion for polemical divinity, is perhaps arguable. But if there is room for it, then More's Dialogue and Tyndale's reply are among the more powerful Christian controversies. More seems for the last time to be relaxed in his writing and surrounds his debate with a fictional setting such as he had written in *Utopia* and rather less successfully in *Rosseus*. There is plenty of humour, some very good stories. More was after all a layman, and while he knew his Fathers and was a considerable philosopher he did not perhaps know how much there was in sixteenth-century theology to support some of Tyndale's distinctions, e.g. about the nature of the Church.

But what he might lack in technical skills, was more than compensated for by his powers of marshalling evidence, of detecting flaws in argument, and by an appeal to humour and common sense such as in our time made G. K. Chesterton, another layman, so irresistible. Above all, he writes as a lawyer, and he reads Tyndale's pages as though they were legal documents, for what they say rather than for what they are intended to mean. This really was warfare where neither side could clearly see the other for the smoke of battle. War with no generosity on either side. It is not our business to appraise or re-appraise the theological debate, which doubtless somebody will one day do, in the light of Vatican II and in the spirit of *De Ecumenismo*. But it is important to understand how More saw his opponents, to realize that when he wrote off Luther as a fool, a sot, a liar and a lecher, it was because he believed that heresy could only result from malice, and from pride, and that he feared the consequences to the salvation of men and nations, if such perverted doctrines should prevail. But if from More's Humpty Dumpty point of view it was only a 'good knock down argument' because words had to mean what the Church had for centuries said they meant, there was no room for concessions, still less for understanding that Luther and Tyndale had a case. None the less, there is great argument and if by now More and Erasmus had retreated from expressing views – More in his letters to Dorp and Batmanson about the new learning, and Erasmus about the open Bible in the introduction to his New Testament – of boldness, the situation, they felt, had changed, and More even said that the early Fathers would have spoken more discreetly had they known how the Reformers would misuse them.

More's second work, his *Confutation* of Tyndale's reply – Part I, 1532, Part II, 1533, is far less successful. For one thing the book was lengthened tediously by his scrupulous method of printing the full text of his opponent. It was perhaps a little hard to reproach Tyndale for not doing the same thing for when a later biographer of More said of Tyndale that he

> was in a labyrinth and many times so brought to bay that he was like to a hare
> that had twenty brace of greyhounds after her

he spoke more truly than he intended and Tyndale driven from pillar to post, always on the run, had no room or time or money for polemical luxuries. More has still some fine passages, good stories, as well as some rather nasty passages and there is an imaginary meditation of an antinomian Reformer thinking evangelical thoughts while committing fornication which if it anticipates James Hogg's 'Justified Sinner' is tasteless and indeed outrageous. But he is, as C. S. Lewis put it:

> monotonously anxious to conquer and to conquer equally at every moment: to show in everything that every heretical book is wrong about everything: wrong in history, in logic and in rhetoric and in English grammar as well as in theology – to rebuke magnificently is one of the duties of a great polemical writer. More often attempts it, but he always fails.

In 1529 More wrote the *Supplication of Souls* in reply to a vitriolic tract by Simon Fish which returned to the old Wycliffite demand for the disendowment of the Church. He wrote a long open letter to the 'young man' John Frith whose views on the eucharist derived from the Basle Reformer Oecolampadius, but who added the revolutionary notion that unanimity about the eucharist ought not to be a matter of life and death. And he became involved with a distinguished lawyer St Germain, about the relation of spiritual and temporal power in his *Apology* . . . and his *Debellation of Salem and Byzance* and replied to a tract *The Supper of the Lord* which may have been the work of George Joye.

More, like most of us, was better at the things he affirmed than those he denied; the Sacrament of the Altar, the Real Presence and the Sacrifice of the Mass; the intercession of the saints, the belief in purgatory. In his reply to Tyndale he put Holy Church over and against Holy Writ, though More himself gave great reverence to scripture while Tyndale believed the great theological and Christological doctrines of the ecumenical creeds. But, with Fisher, More believed that there were many things of faith and practice which were not mentioned in the New Testament, and which had been handed down from the apostles in unwritten form. And when, as he believed, these things had been accepted by holy Fathers, and taught for a thousand years, he refused to disobey this 'common sense of the faithful'. For like his friend Erasmus he laid great stress on this common and accepted belief of Christendom. The marble slab in Canterbury over More's remains bears the words from Magna Carta – *Ecclesia Anglicana libera sit* – let the English Church be free! More himself like John Henry Newman after him, might have thought even more apt the great saying of Augustine, *securus judicat orbis terrarum*. – 'the world is safe when it judges!'.

In a decade of controversy I do not think More changed his mind very much about the authority of the Pope, though he came to think of the papacy as more than a human contrivance, and though he did, as he himself said, write very little about the power of the Pope, left the canon lawyers to talk about the papal plenitude of power, and never regarded the Pope as above a General Council.

It is perhaps significant that his long polemical debate tails off without conclusion in the midst of a discussion of the tract of Robert Barnes – 'What the church is – and who be there'. For perhaps the long hours of meditation and writing confirmed him above all in his belief about the Catholic Church. He did not deny that the Church is a communion of saints, but he refused, unlike his opponents, to drive a wedge between that mystical fellowship and the concrete, empirical, juridical existence of the Catholic Church throughout the Christian world. This is the Church whose authority he accepts and he was prepared to think with this Church and to obey it. But it was in these very months that he saw one part of this Catholic Church moving towards schism, towards the repudiation of all those ties, spiritual, juridical, political, financial which bound Christendom together, under the leadership of that Bishop of Rome, to whom as the successor of St Peter a divine commission of oversight had been given. It is an interesting thought that More was publicly writing page after page in the defence of this view of the Church at a time when he kept closely to himself his own opinion about the actions of his King and of his King's government, yet it was really this conception of the Church and its authority which brought him to his death.

More did not, we have seen, confine his action to reading and writing. When he became Lord Chancellor, he stepped up his action against heretics:

> seeing the King's gracious purpose in this point: I reckon that being his unworthy chancellor it appertaineth as I said unto my part and duty – with opening to his people the malice and poison of those pernicious books . . . by mine office in virtue of mine oath and every officer of justice through the realm for his rate, right especially bounden not in reason only and good congruence but also by plain ordinance and statute.

When the Basle Reformer Simon Grynaeus wished to visit England, on the search for manuscripts, he got Erasmus to recommend him, and More promised to receive him. Grynaeus was a distinguished New Testament scholar and a very nice man, but More was taking no chances. He gave him the superior KGB treatment, never letting his guest out of sight of himself or his secretary, John Harris. Grynaeus was either very innocent, which is not probable, or he knew what was going on, and in his 'Thank you' letter which took the form of a postponed dedication to John More, he thanked More for such close personal attention and for once out-ironied More.

More's garden at Chelsea came to seem a sinister place to the Reformers, and the new building acquired a lock up and a set of stocks. When More could, he reasoned with suspects, but if they were obdurate he handed them over to the spiritual arm, though in some cases they came back to Chelsea for their sentence. This happened to the London mercer, Tewkesbury, and to the Middle Temple lawyer, Bainham, and since on one occasion More's lawyer sons-in-law, Roper and Dauncey are named among those present (and when we remember Rastell's visit to Frith in the Tower) we may wonder if a More team did not go to work. More was never cruel, but he could be severe and he could look on at harsh treatment administered by others on those he regarded as worse than murderers or thieves.

It is sometimes said that there was nothing personal about his hatred for heretics, as if that were not what every terrorist says as he plants a bomb. And if More's writings against Luther lacked any personal encounter he did meet a number of English heretics. Not perhaps the best kind, for they were often like George Constantine and William Barlow, those who had abjured their heresy. And in the 1520s the Cambridge dons, like their Oxford counterparts in the time of Wycliffe showed that their dissent turned to abjuration rather than martyrdom when the crunch came. But there was a new toughness coming, as perhaps More sensed with the young John Frith. There is not much evidence that More softened towards these men, save for one startling and prophetic sentence:

And yet Son Roper, I pray God that some of us, high as we seem to sit upon the mountains treading heretics under our feet like ants, live not to see the day that we would gladly be at league and composition with those whom you call heretics to let them have their churches quietly to themselves so that they would be content to let us have ours quietly to ourselves.

Under our feet. Like ants. But they were men.

The Reformation Parliament

Almost from the beginning of his Chancellorship events began to move in the direction More most feared. 'If the lion knew his strength, hard were it for any man to rule him' was a remark More made to Thomas Cromwell. And it became plain that the lion was already testing his claws. It seems that Henry by 1529 was no longer only concerned to get his divorce, but that he was wondering whether he might not throw off the whole Roman obedience and exercise his own paramount authority as a Christian prince within the Empire of England.

The Reformation parliament met in Blackfriars, 3 November 1529, and in his speech More was obliged to make some mention of the fallen Cardinal, whom he referred to contemptuously as the 'great wether which is of late fallen, so craftily, so scabbily, yea and so untruly juggled with the king'. Almost immediately the Commons petitioned the King against the spiritual abuse of power by the clergy, and this took shape in a collection of anticlerical bills. When they reached the Lords, they provoked an outspoken and courageous speech by John Fisher against those who cried 'down with the Church', and in which he pointed the parallel with Bohemia, the land of heresy, and denounced those who wanted not the good but the goods of the Church. The Commons were outraged, and Henry and his government added this speech to the now long list of checks this turbulent priest had put in their way. Now, after the example of Wolsey, the whole clergy were charged with breach of Praemunire, and though they were let off with a vast fine, they had ominously to accord the King the title of 'Supreme Head of the Church as far as the laws of Christ allow'.

Resignation

The King had submitted the divorce question to the learned men of the Universities of France and Italy, after having successfully browbeaten the Universities of Oxford and Cambridge. The royal emissaries argued and bribed their way from city to city and succeeded in winning favourable judgements from eight Universities of varying reputation (but they included Paris and Bologna), and of varying quality (one or two dodged the problem of the impediment of moral law, and another assumed the consummation of Arthur's marriage). These were forwarded to the Pope who was not at all impressed.

They were now read to Parliament by Sir Brian Tuke in the context of a speech by More in which he declared the sincerity of the King's intentions. There was an awkward moment when somebody demanded to know More's opinion, but he shrugged it off with the statement that the King already knew what he thought. The next day Parliament was adjourned, and did not meet again until 1532. When it did the Commons returned at once to their anticleric grievances, and to the document which had been taking shape since 1529, the 'Supplication against the Ordinaries', to which the Convocation sent a bold reply. In return, on 10 May the clergy were faced with extreme demands by the King: chief among them all future ecclesiastical legislation must receive the King's consent. And though several bishops fought boldly to the last, the lower House of Convocation and a small rump minority of bishops surrendered on 15 May. On the following day, More resigned his Chancellorship. The approximation of the dates is, as they say, coincidental, for the resignation must have been long contemplated, and steps taken to approach the King, some time before.

More had lain awake o'nights when Dame Alice slept, pondering what might happen, and the consequences to himself, taking the thoughts to their almost unbearable and cruel conclusion. Not only cowards, but the men of sensitive hearts and high imagination die many times before their death.

But the King still made gracious remarks and saw to it that the Duke of Norfolk publicly paid tribute to More, and disposed of the rumour that he had been forced to resign. More himself had pleaded ill health and there is no reason to doubt that at this time he began to suffer from internal pain. But knowing More we may wonder if there was not a deliberate ambivalence in his letter to Erasmus 'I am suffering from pains in the chest [but the word is *pectus* – which could mean 'heart' and even 'conscience']' and he went on to say that the doctors said it was going to be a long business ('and I don't know whether I shall come out of it alive'). More had lost his livelihood at a stroke. And at a family council of war he joked about the need to tighten their belts (he found his jester a place with his father, and his watermen were employed by his successor) and contemplated a gradual descent in life style so that if all else failed –

Then may we yet, with bags and wallets, go a begging together, and hoping that for pity some good folk will give us their charity at everyman's door to sing 'Salve Regina' and so still keep company and be merry together.

If there was no new income, More could live off his hump for some time, and his sons-in-law could keep them from penury. They were able to stay at Chelsea.

There is the splendid, credible story of how gently More broke to Lady Alice the fact that they had come down in the world:

And whereas upon the holidays during his high Chancellorship, when the service at the church was done, one of his gentlemen ordinarily used to come to my lady his wife's pew and say unto her 'Madam, my lord is gone', the next holiday after the surrender of his office he came unto my lady his wife's pew himself, and making a low courtesy said unto her 'Madam, my lord is gone'.

Redundant, retired, More began to feel his age, and he sent Erasmus a copy of the epitaph he intended to have inscribed on his memorial in Chelsea church. He goes out of his way to praise Henry VIII:

He was admitted to the Court by the invincible Henry the Eighth, who is the only King ever to have received the unique distinction of meriting the title 'Defender of the Faith', a title earned by deeds of sword and pen.

Alone of his embassies he selected the Peace of Cambrai for mention, 'may heaven confirm this peace and make it a lasting one'. He claimed only this for himself that

his excellent sovereign found no fault with his service, neither did he make himself odious to the nobles nor unpleasant to the populace, but he was a source of trouble to thieves, murderers and heretics.

He added a loving eulogy of his father, and the hope that now, in his retirement, he Thomas More might reach 'the object of his longing – to have the last years of his life all to himself, so that he could gradually retire from the affairs of this world and contemplate the eternity of the life to come'.

There was attached an epitaph to his first 'little wife' and to his second who 'has been as devoted to her stepchildren (a rare attainment in a stepmother as very few mothers are to their own children)'.

Tunstall raised a great collection, perhaps between four and five thousand pounds and offered it to More on behalf of the clergy, as token of their gratitude for his defence of Christian truth. But More was genuinely shocked at the thought of taking money for what he had accepted as a God given task, and refused. He may also have known that it would give handle to the charge, already made by Tyndale and others, that he was covetous. Nor was this the moment in time to be accepting great presents from the English clergy. But he seems to have spent the next year safely and quietly, reading and writing out his great arguments.

'Many and Great Dangers'

In 1533 political events began once more to move. The new Archbishop of Canterbury, Thomas Cranmer, cited Catherine and Henry to a special court held at Dunstable a few miles from her dwelling and on 23 May pronounced the marriage between Catherine and Henry illicit and invalid.

At some time during this period, Henry and Anne had been married by Edward Lee, Archbishop of York and on 28 May at a special tribunal at Lambeth Cranmer declared that marriage 'true, pure and legitimate'. Speed had been essential, for the coronation was to be on 1 June.

Three bishops, Tunstall, Clerk and Gardiner invited More to go to the coronation with them, and sent him twenty pounds towards a new gown. He jokingly kept the gift but he refused to attend the coronation and though few could have noticed his absence from the junketings, no doubt his absence was remarked and reported in high places.

Now More had to walk delicately. He at some time took steps to see that his property was distributed among his children, and made Margaret and Roper a gift outright, the only one which eventually and after his attainder, was allowed to stand. Unlike Fisher who had committed himself again and again in speech and writing, More had written not a word.

When the Emperor Charles V wrote to him, he refused to touch the letter when it was proffered him by Chapuys, the ambassador. It became clear that there were those who were not minded to allow More to fade quietly out of national life. An attempt to prove that he had taken bribes collapsed with the plain proof to the contrary.

The Nun of Kent

Then, out of the blue, a dangerous situation arose. Elizabeth Barton, a serving maid at Aldington in Kent, began to see visions and speak prophecies, to the accompaniment of strange physical symptoms (perhaps of an epileptic kind). She began so to behave in 1525 and became the centre of a local cult, the fame of which came to John Fisher, Cardinal Wolsey and Archbishop Warham, who interviewed her. She was attended by a group of clergy, secular and religious, who were later accused, perhaps unjustly, of manipulating her opinion. Despite her later confession of fraud, it is not certain that she did not genuinely believe in her visions.

There were many such visionaries with followings in sixteenth-century Europe and often little to tell, by sifting popular gossip, whether a woman was a Margery Kempe or Lady Julian, or a hysterical impostor, or a lunatic. She began to move around, claimed to be at Calais when Henry and Anne Boleyn were there, and she visited the friars at Sion. Though Catherine of Aragon wisely refused to see her, those who most befriended her were of the Queen's party and matters took a deadly turn when she began to speak against the divorce and to threaten Henry that divine wrath would take away his throne. What she said was no doubt what many people were saying in their cups, but popular gossip was one thing, a claim to divine inspiration another. Less heady stuff from a friar had brought the Duke of Buckingham to the scaffold in recent memory. Who was to say whether Elizabeth Barton was a wild woman like Helen of Tottenham, or like that other serving maid, Joan of Orleans, able to raise war?

Once again, Fisher was in trouble. He had believed that Elizabeth Barton was genuine, and her claim to have received a letter from Saint Mary Magdalene intrigued him, for it had been one of his hobbies to disentangle the 'Marys' of the New Testament. He had listened to all she had to say, and he had not passed her sayings about the divorce on to the King, which brought him in danger of 'misprision of treason'.

But More, too, had visited the woman and had written her a letter. This her inquisitors discovered. After a public penance at Paul's Cross and Canterbury, the Maid and her clerical sponsors were attainted in February 1534 and the names of Fisher and More included in the Act of Attainder. This moved More to immediate action and he at once sent a long letter to Cromwell, with a complete statement about all his dealings with the Nun of Kent, including a copy of his letter to her, which he had prudently retained.

In his letter More had warned her that

Many folks desire to speak with you, which are not all peradventure of my mind . . . but some hap to be curious and inquisitive of things that little pertain to their parts:

I nothing doubt your wisdom and the spirit of God shall keep you from talking with any persons, especially with lay persons of such manner things as pertain to princes' affairs or the state of the realm.

More told Cromwell that when, about 1526, the King first had news about her visions, he had asked More what he thought about it all, but he had replied

I durst not nor would not be bold in judging the matter.

Others were more credulous, and More told how he had been visited at Chelsea by Father Resby of the Friars Observant at Canterbury and Father Rich of the Observants of Sheen on two separate occasions, both having been enthusiastic about the Maid, so that More had to check them, refusing to hear a word about her political prophesying. But on a visit to Sheen, More had heard from the brothers that they were worried about her, and he had later returned for an interview with her in which he gave her kindly warning, and when

my time came to go home, I gave her a double ducat and prayed her to pray for me and mine.

But More made a point of being present at Paul's Cross when the Maid confessed to being an impostor and he had immediately sent word to the Proctor of the Charterhouse 'that she was undoubtedly proved a false, deceiving hypocrite'.

It was a good defence, though Cromwell, trying to keep track of the Queen's party, must have noted the kind of clergy who stayed at More's house, and the kind of religious he was wont to visit – all associated with the Queen's cause. Elizabeth Barton and her attendant clergy were executed. It must have been an enormous relief to More when his name was taken out of the Bill, and he thought

Anno 1505 29 october ꝺmaga henzirh vij braurigz zrge illuſtziſſimu ozdmata ꝑ hezmaun zmrk ꝛo zegie ... uiberium · :·

The Armes of the Worshipfull
Companey of the Mercers:

Hen: St george: Richmond

... quantum ... de sideriorum seren...
... Marcutius de Gorenodo haro Montanerz et Ma...

... cius consorz Regina cum sue comitatibus ibunt in districtum et dominum dicti serenissimi Romanorum et hi...
et hispanorum Rex ac illustrissima domina Margareta amita sua cum sue comitatibus dement in districtum et ...
t aut manserint respective panformiter dabitur Conventum qua fortasse continget duos principes exertis supradicto uti...
onte dicto Regum conventu diligenter observandas concordatum et conclusum est die undecimo iulii supradicto uti...
didam Athesiam et Angliam exploranda et speculanda Et si quos suspectos repererint arcendos et amonendos vi...
ortione molestia inquietudinestur et secure accedere et recedere valeant Teneantur dicti exploratores singulis du...
redicte qz omnes exercitus seu gentes armorum huiusde qz parte utriusqz Principis Iosephi ... pro presidio ...
stantes et armoti et nec ipsi ise aliqua aliqui durante dictorum Regum conventu proprius accedere quomodo presumant.
... Reges confirmabuntur omy reliquiis articulis presentis tractatus

Item

Paceus ♌

Thomas More

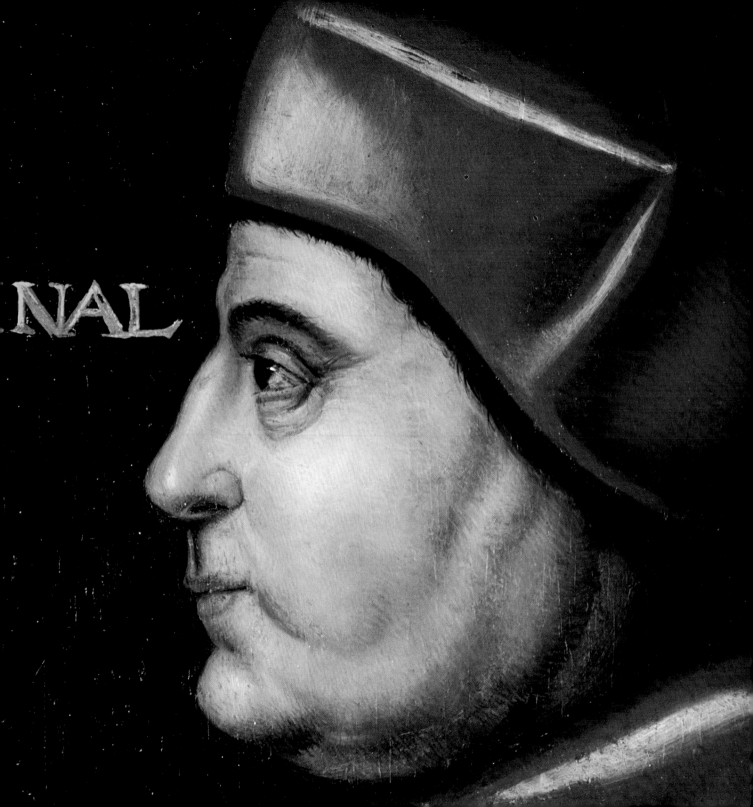

The Armes of the Worshipfull
Companey of the Mercers:

Hen: St george. Richmond

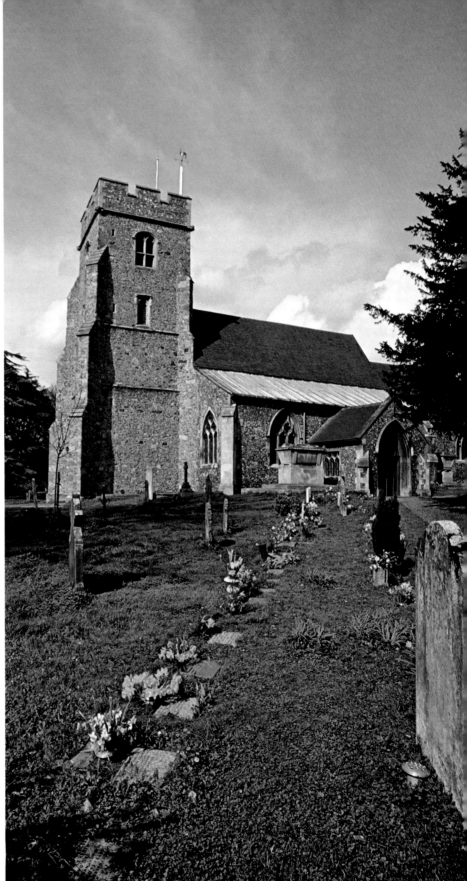

... in nobis est huiusmodi ...
... de Correnodo haro Montancey ...

... eius consort Regina cum suis comitatibus ibunt in districtum et dominium dicti serenissimi Pontanorum et
... Hispaniarum Rex ac illustrissima domina Margareta amita sua cum suis comitatibus veniet in districtum eorum proce-
... aut manserint respective conformiter dabitur. Item quia forsasse continget duos principes eorum proce-
noctis, siue interdum libere ficri possint. Conuentum concordatum et conclusum est die vndecimo Julii supradicto ...
... dicto Regina conuentu diligenter obseruandas. An quidem nobiles eius sui comitiua speculatores et explor-
... molestia inquietudine sine et secure accedere et recedere valeant. Et si quos suspectos repererint explorat-
... omnes armatis seu gentes armorum huiunde ex parte vtriusque Principis ... militibus pro pr-
... Reges confirmabuntur cum zeliquis articulis presentis tractatus ... conuentu propius accedere quomodo presum-

Paceus

Thomas More

1907

NAL

Picture Index

1 The wrought iron rose in the screen at Hampton Court, which was built 1514–26 by Cardinal Wolsey. The rose was the symbol of the rival houses of Lancaster (the red rose) and York (the white rose), who fought the Wars of the Roses (1455–85) as rival claimants for the English throne. The war ended with the defeat and death of the Yorkist Richard III at the Battle of Bosworth and an end was put to the rivalry of the two houses by the marriage of Henry Tudor of Lancaster to Elizabeth of York in 1486.

2 The Round Tower, Windsor Castle. The castle was originally built by William the Conqueror in 1070, but was rebuilt and enlarged with additional towers and a keep by Edward III. Subsequently added to and rebuilt by Elizabeth I and George IV, Windsor Castle, the largest inhabited castle in the world, is one of the principal residences of the British royal family.

4 Tower Bridge (opened in 1894), which crosses the River Thames near the Tower of London, is the dominant feature in this view of the City of London. The photograph was taken from the Monument, a stone column built by Christopher Wren to commemorate the Great Fire of London, which in 1666 devastated a wide area of the City.

3 Henry VII. The son of Edmund Tudor, Earl of Richmond, he assumed the crown of England after he had defeated Richard III at Bosworth. A firm and prudent man, he ruled England from 1485 to 1509. Artist unknown, 1505. National Portrait Gallery.

5 Morton House in Hatfield, Hertfordshire, the summer residence of John Morton, Archbishop of Canterbury, who in 1490 took the young Thomas More into his household to train as a page.

6 Old oak trees standing in the grounds of Morton House.

7 Morton's Tower, which forms the entrance to Lambeth Palace, the London residence of the Archbishop of Canterbury, Primate of all England. The Tower, which was named after Thomas More's patron, was built in 1490, although the Palace itself dates from the end of the twelfth century.

11 A corridor at Charterhouse, originally a Carthusian monastery in London, where Thomas More is reputed to have often visited in order to fast and pray. Founded in 1371, it was dissolved during the Reformation, and later a hospital and a school were founded on the site.

8 The inner courtyard of Christ Church, Oxford, founded by Cardinal Wolsey in 1525. The largest of the Oxford colleges, it absorbed Canterbury College, at which Thomas More may have studied from 1492 to 1494.

12 Sixteenth-century timber-frame houses at Staple Inn, London. It was here that Henry V (1387-1422) built one of the nine London Inns of Chancery, a law school which students had to attend before they could complete their studies at one of the Inns of Court.

9 Thomas More. Detail from a miniature (1532–34) by Hans Holbein the Younger. Lincoln's Inn, London.

13 The coat of arms of the Mercers' Company. Started as a group of London mercers (dealers in textile fabrics) in the twelfth century, and instituted as a Guild in 1393, this was the most important and the richest of all the City Guilds. As a young lawyer, More frequently represented the Mercers, of which he became a Freeman in 1509. The Arms are situated in the Mercers' Hall, which was rebuilt traditionally after being blitzed during World War II.

10 A view of the garden of Lincoln's Inn, one of the four Inns of Court in London. These four voluntary societies, which were originated in the thirteenth century, possess the exclusive right to call candidates to the English Bar. Thomas More is thought to have practised here from about 1495.

14 The Great Hall of the London Guildhall, the meeting-place of the City Corporation, which also contains a library, a museum and an art gallery, and which dates from the fifteenth century. The decorations are the coats of arms of the twelve great City Guilds (at the rear, left, is the flag of the Mercers' Company). As Under-Sheriff of London, Thomas More often worked at Guildhall.

15   Detail from a portrait of Thomas More by an unknown artist. Private collection, London.

19   Henry VIII (1491-1547), aged about 30. A detail from a portrait by an unknown artist. National Portrait Gallery, London.

16   English pastoral scene in Hertfordshire, not far from the country seat of the More family at Gobions, North Mimms. According to the family tradition it was here that Thomas More wrote the first part of *Utopia*.

20   Catherine of Aragon (1485-1536), first wife of Henry VIII. The daughter of Ferdinand and Isabella of Spain, Catherine was the widow of Henry's brother Arthur when they married in 1509. Eighteen years later, after Catherine had failed to provide him with a male heir, Henry divorced her on the grounds that she had formerly been his brother's wife. The refusal of the Pope to sanction this divorce led to the final rupture of the Church of England from the Church of Rome, as well as the downfall of Thomas More. Painted by an unknown artist. National Portrait Gallery, London.

17   Peter Gilles (Peter Aegidius) of Antwerp, with a letter from Thomas More in his hand. The painting is by Quentin Metsys, and the letter probably concerns a portrait of Erasmus which the artist had painted as a present for More. Museum vor schoone Kunsten, Antwerp.

18   Erasmus of Rotterdam by Hans Holbein the Younger (1530). Desiderius Erasmus (c.1466–1536) was the most famous scholar in Northern Europe, and a great friend of Thomas More, with whom he collaborated in humanist enterprises. Though deeply critical of the church life of his day, he opposed the Reformation on account of its destructive violence.

21   Thomas More with his family. Watercolour sketch by Rowland Locky (c. 1590) after the painting by Hans Holbein the Younger (1527). Victoria and Albert Museum, London.

22 St Mary's Church at North Mimms near the More family estate.

26. The silver seal of Thomas More, with the family arms, showing the crest as a Moor's head. Stonyhurst College, near Blackburn, Lancashire.

23 Crosby Hall in Chelsea, London, is a good example of late-fifteenth century English architecture. It was owned briefly by Thomas More (1523-4) when it stood on its original site in Bishopsgate. Subsequently it was moved stone by stone to its present site in Danvers Street.

27 The thirteenth-century Market Halls at Bruges are overlooked by an 80 metres high belfry in which is a famous carillon of 49 bells.

24 The River Thames at Chelsea. Little remains today of the Chelsea of Thomas More's time – even his beloved garden, which stretched from his house to the Thames, has been built over. As was common in Tudor England, the Thames was More's favourite way of getting from Chelsea to the City of London.

28 Document of an agreement between the English and the Holy Roman Emperor, Charles V, dated 14 July 1520, which bears the signature of Thomas More, acting on Henry VIII's behalf. Service d'Archives, Lille.

25 The More Chapel in Old Church Chelsea, once the Parish church of Chelsea. The epitaph on the wall was composed by More. The chapel, which survived bombing during World War II, was originally built by More in 1532 and it was his intention that both his first and second wife should be buried there, at his side. He was however executed as a traitor and buried in the chapel of St Peter ad Vincula in the Tower (his head was buried at St Dunstan's, Canterbury).

29 Cardinal Thomas Wolsey (c. 1473-1530). In 1515 Wolsey was created Cardinal and Lord Chancellor by Henry VIII, but his failure to arrange Henry's divorce from Catherine of Aragon led to his dismissal and arrest. Detail from a painting by an unknown artist. National Portrait Gallery, London.

30 The West front and main entrance of the palace at Hampton Court. Built between 1514 and 1526 by Cardinal Wolsey, who presented it to Henry VIII in 1528 in an attempt to regain the king's favour. The palace which was enlarged by Henry, and later partially renewed by Christopher Wren in the seventeenth century, contains about 1,000 rooms, art treasures, and fine gardens.

31 Henry VIII, accompanied by Thomas More, Cardinal Wolsey and Bishop John Fisher, on his way to his meeting with François I of France on the 'Field of the Cloth of Gold' near Arras in June 1520. The interview between the two monarchs was so-called due to the magnificence displayed by the two kings and their retinue. Lord Chamberlain's Office, London (copyright reserved).

32 François I, King of France (1494-1547; reigned 1515-47). Detail from the painting by Jean Clouet (?) (c. 1540). Uffizi, Florence.

33 Martin Luther, the German religious leader (1483-1546). An Augustinian friar, he was excommunicated in 1521 after he had initiated the Protestant Reformation by campaigning against the sale of indulgencies. Painting by Lucas Cranach the Elder. Herzoy Anton Ulrich Museum, Braunschweig.

34 Pope Leo X (Pope 1513-21), with Cardinals Giulio de' Medici and Luigi de' Rossi. It was Leo's issue of indulgencies to raise funds for the rebuilding of St Peter's that aroused the indignation of Martin Luther. Painting by Raphael (1514). Palazzo Pitti, Florence.

35 Henry VIII. A painting by Hans Holbein the Younger (1536-7). Thyssen Collection, Lugano.

36 A 'Golden Rose' similar to those which, since the eleventh century, the Popes have consecrated on the fourth Sunday in Lent (Laetare), and then sent to worthy persons as a mark of honour. On 11 October 1521, after Henry VIII's letter denouncing Luther, *Assertio Septem Sacramentorum,* Pope Leo X bestowed on Henry the title 'Defender of the Faith'. Musée de Cluny, Paris.

37 Thomas More as Lord Chancellor. Painted in 1527 by Hans Holbein the Younger, this is one of the finest of Holbein's portraits of Thomas More. Frick Collection, New York.

41 It was in this room in the Bell Tower at the Tower of London that Thomas More spent the fifteen months from his arrest to his execution.

38 The nucleus of the buildings which comprise the Tower of London is the White Tower, the keep of the original fortress, built c. 1078 by William the Conqueror. The tower, which also contains the beautiful Chapel of St John, is today a museum of armour and weapons.

42 Thomas Cranmer (1489-1556), Archbishop of Canterbury from 1532. He gained the favour of Henry VIII by writing in defence of Henry's divorce from Catherine and was sent to argue on behalf of it in Italian Universities and before the Pope. On his return from Rome he was elevated to the Archbishopric and from then on, he furthered the cause of the Reformation, in securing the authorisation of the English Bible, and in liturgical studies which culminated in the Book of Common Prayer. It was Cranmer who pronounced Henry's divorce from Catherine and confirmed his marriage to Anne Boleyn. He was one of the few who kept the trust and friendship of Henry VIII to the end. On the accession of Henry's eldest daughter Mary, he was imprisoned and burned at Oxford in 1556. Detail from a painting by G. Flicke. National Portrait Gallery, London.

39 Henry VIII in his wedding outfit, aged 49. Painted in 1540 by Hans Holbein the Younger. National Gallery, Rome.

40 Anne Boleyn (c. 1507-36), the second wife of Henry VIII and mother of Elizabeth I. A maid of honour to Catherine of Aragon, she attracted the admiration of Henry, who then determined to divorce Catherine. Anne's marriage to Henry became the primary cause for the downfall and death of Thomas More. However, Anne herself only outlived More by one year, being beheaded at the Tower on a charge of adultery and conspiracy in 1536. Painting by an unknown artist. National Portrait Gallery, London.

43 Pope Clement VII (Pope 1523-34). He refused to sanction the divorce between Henry VIII and Catherine of Aragon which ultimately caused the schism between England and the Holy See. Painted in 1526 by Sebastian Piombo. Museo Capadimonte, Naples.

44 Westminster Hall was the scene of the trial of Thomas More in 1535. The Hall is attached to the Houses of Parliament at Westminster and was built by William II and roofed and remodelled by Richard II. It is the oldest surviving part of the medieval Palace of Westminster and from the thirteenth to the nineteenth century it served as the highest English law court. It is especially celebrated for its roof, which is made of thirteen great timber beams, and is one of the largest in the world to be unsupported.

48 The execution block and axe at the Tower of London.

45 Pope Paul III (Pope 1534-49) with his 'nephews' Ottavio and Cardinal Alessandro Farnese. It was his nomination of Bishop John Fisher as a Cardinal in, 1535 that so angered Henry VIII that he allowed the executions of Fisher and Thomas More to be expedited. He also caused Henry to be excommunicated from the Catholic Church in 1536. Painted by Titian in 1546. Museo Capodimonte, Naples.

49 The Church of St Dunstan (dating from the fourteenth-fifteenth century) in Canterbury. Thomas More's head, which was saved by his daughter Margaret, has rested since at least 1585 in the Roper family vault here. An ecumenical service is held in this Anglican church every year on the anniversary of More's death. More's bones are believed to have been interred in the Chapel of St Peter ad Vincula in the Tower of London.

46 Thomas More in prison, holding the red wooden cross, which he carried with him to his execution. Together with picture no. 15, this portrait forms a diptych, which is privately owned by Mr Thomas Eyston, a descendent of the More family. Henred House, Wantage, Berkshire.

50 St George fighting the dragon. A gold and enamelled medallion, formerly containing a miniature of Thomas More. On the other side of the medallion is a Resurrection scene with Christ seated on an empty tomb. This relic of More's dating from the mid-sixteenth century is preserved at Stonyhurst College, Lancashire.

47 Margaret More (1505-1544), the eldest daughter of Thomas More, who married William Roper, the biographer of her father. A detail from the family portrait painted for More's grandson Thomas in 1593, after Hans Holbein's family picture. National Portrait Gallery, London.

he owed something to Cromwell and to Lord Audley who persuaded the King that More must not be allowed to address the Lords.

The Prisoner of Conscience

On 5 March 1534 More wrote two letters. The one was to the King affirming his loyalty. The other, to Cromwell, set out more plainly than he was ever to do again in writing, his attitude to the royal marriage, to the authority of the Church, and of the Pope. Indeed there are some lines which come so near to what the King wished that Rastell omitted them from his edition of More's works.

so am I he that among his Grace's faithful subjects, His highness being in possession of his marriage and this noble woman really anointed Queen, neither murmur at it nor dispute upon it, nor ever did nor will, but without any further meddling of the matter among his faithful subjects faithfully pray for his Grace and hers both, long to live and well, and their noble issue too.

More defended himself against the charge of magnifying papal authority for he had even cut out of a polemical work a section dealing with it. But though he claims that he 'never thought the Pope above the general council' – 'sith Christendom is one corps I cannot perceive how any member thereof may without the common assent of the body, depart from the common head.'

It is a plain statement of views which he did not change, and for which in the end, he died. But when he wrote this letter it was not treason. The situation was rapidly to change. Parliament passed a Succession Act to be promulgated on 1 May 1534. It settled the throne on Henry's eldest surviving son: failing him, on Anne's daughter Elizabeth. But the preamble of the Act was a long repudiation of Catherine and of the jurisdiction of Rome, and deadly sanctions were to be imposed on those who refused to take the oath which was now to be imposed: Those who by writing or action imperilled the life of the King or brought about disturbance against the Crown were guilty of high treason: those who spoke words against the King or his marriage were held guilty of misprision of treason and were to forfeit all their property and be condemned to prison.

More saw that with the imposition of oaths, the crisis was upon him. After a sermon at St Paul's on 12 April 1534 he went to lunch at Bucklersbury with John and Margaret Clement who were living there. A messenger appeared with a summons for him to appear the following day at Lambeth to take the oath. He returned home at once, and the next morning, did what he did in any critical moment, went to church to be confessed and hear Mass –

And whereas he evermore used before at his departure from his wife and children, whom he tenderly loved, to have them bring him to his boat and there to kiss them all and bid them farewell, then would he suffer none of them forth of the gate to follow him, but pulled the wicket after him and with a heavy heart, as by his countenance he appeared, with me and our four servants there he took his boat towards Lambeth. Wherein sitting still sadly awhile at last he suddenly rounded me in the ear, and said 'Son Roper, I thank our Lord the field is won'.

More wrote to Margaret Roper a vivid account of what happened when he appeared before a commission which included the Archbishop of Canterbury, and the Lord Chancellor, the Abbot of Westminster and Thomas Cromwell.

There was a small clerical queue waiting ahead of him, but More, the only layman present, was called in first. He asked to see the oath and that he might read through the Act of Succession and this was granted him. Then More said that while he would not judge others who could take the oath:

Yet unto the oath that there was offered unto me I could not swear, without the jeopardizing of my soul to perpetual damnation.

The Lord Chancellor showed him the long list of Lords and Commons who had already sworn and

I was commanded to go down into the garden and thereupon I tarried in the old burned garden and would not go down because of the heat.

There is an unwonted bitterness in this letter of More in which he described to his daughter the succession of those who went in to swear, and of Dr Nicholas Wilson who was led off to the Tower for refusing: of seeing Hugh Latimer 'very merry for he laughed and took one or twain about the neck so handsomely that if they had been women I would have weened he had been waxen wanton': and the Vicar of Croydon who had after all got no nearer Utopia than free beer at the Archbishop's buttery. And Archbishop Cranmer tried a sophistic quibble.

PART FOUR

'For All Seasons'—*Winter*

Thomas More's Prayer
Book. This *Book of Hours*
printed in Paris, was
among More's posses-
sions in the Tower of
London. It contains his
famous lines 'Godly
Meditation' which
commence: 'Give me
thy grace good lord
to sett the world at
nought...' THE BEINECKE
RARE BOOK AND
MANUSCRIPT LIBRARY,
YALE UNIVERSITY.

52

Cranmer afterwards attempted to save More, by suggesting that he might swear the oath to the succession, but not the preamble or the statute as a whole – perhaps Cromwell would have gone along with this, but the King was by now implacable.

More needed to defend himself against the charge of obstinacy. He said that if the King would give him commission under Letters Patent, he would write down the reasons for his refusal – but only if assured they would not be used as evidence against him. Cromwell told him this was legally impossible. More then ended where he had begun, by saying that he accused nobody:

I never withdrew any man from it, nor never advised any to refuse it, nor never put nor will, any scruple in any mans head, but leave every man to his own conscience. And methinketh in good faith that so it were good reason that every man should leave me to mine.

He was put in the custody of the Abbot of Westminster and four days later was escorted as a prisoner to the Tower, 17 April 1534.

He had to be talked out of wearing his precious chain which marked him as 'the King's good servant' on the grounds that it would inevitably be filched from him. But it was a serious gesture. We shall never understand why More refused to swear the oath, unless we remember how solemn and important was the oath he had already sworn, of loyalty and obedience to his King that godly Prince whom he esteemed perhaps a little more than did Thomas Cromwell and only a little less than did Thomas Cranmer.

Visitors to the Tower today are shown a reconstructed cell where rats gnaw at the feet of dirty prisoners in filthy straw. But More, either in the Bell or Beauchamp Tower, was given what we would today call VIP treatment. His cell was roomy enough, and he was allowed a manservant, though the cost of their board and lodging became a heavy expense for Lady Alice. He was allowed a visit or two from Meg and from his wife, and they were permitted to stroll and talk in the garden.

Will Roper (was he perhaps given to imitations of his mother-in-law?) gives the unforgettable picture of one conversation. When his wife reproached him

What in God's name you mean to tarry here? – with a cheerful countenance he said to her – Mrs Alice, tell me one thing. 'What is that', quoth she? Is not this house as near heaven as my own? Whereto after her accustomed homely fashion she answered – 'Tille valle, tille valle – *bone deus, bone deus* man, will your old tricks never be left?'

But More was putting the best face on things and when she heard the gaoler's key turn in the lock, she exclaimed! It was really no answer when More teasingly reminded her that every night she not only locked the doors, but the windows.

For he knew, and she knew, the traumatic meaning of being locked in prison.

More's Last Writings

For a time More had his books and his writing materials: now he concentrated on the edifying writings he had maybe begun at home, the short English homilies *On the Passion* – the extended treatise *Dialogue of Comfort* – a tract on *To receive the Blessed Body* and a final meditation in Latin *De Tristitia Christi*.

It would be impertinent, in every sense of the word, to comment on the literary quality of these last writings, or try to assess their place in the comparative history of spirituality. The *Dialogue of Comfort* is indeed full of comfortable words and has solaced many. The fictional, dialogue device sounds a little weary – Hungary (with the Turks at the gates!) – far away, and yet so close. But it has noble passages including a lovely exposition of the 90 (91) Psalm. The other writings illustrate, not only More's devotion to the Blessed Sacrament, but that 'theology of the Cross' which marks late medieval European devotion.

Utopia, we saw, began with a famous literary setting, a group of friends talking in a garden. Now in his *Tristitia Christi* More turns to another garden, and another group of friends, Jesus and the disciples in Gethsemane. It is all about the impending passion of Jesus. It is also all about Thomas More.

His two prayer books, with their scattered jottings, take us to the heart of the matter. His Latin Psalter – for the Psalms take on another dimension in a prisoner situation – with the frequent mention of the phrase *pro rege* shows that More continued to pray for his King (was not David a most famous godly Prince?). But the most frequent comment, written scores of times is the word 'Demons' – *Demones*, and it comes at places where the reference is obviously to men, to enemies and liars and betrayers. In these last weeks he was fighting for his soul, not against flesh and blood but against principalities and powers. For all his friends had come to doubt his wisdom. Erasmus was to make the cold comment 'he should not have got entangled in dangerous affairs and he ought to have left theology to the theologians'. Even his daughter seems not to have fully understood, and added her voice to get his wry smile – 'you, too, Mother Eve?' At the top and bottom of his other book, his *Book of Hours of Our Lady* he wrote lines of a prayer, and these begin

Give me thy grace good Lord
To set the world at nought
To set my mind fast upon thee

And not to hang upon the blast of men's mouths.

Save for Fisher, almost all of More's friends had sworn the oath, and began to draw away from him. 'By the Mass, Master More', warned the Duke of Norfolk, 'it is perilous striving with Princes. And therefore I would wish you somewhat to incline to the King's pleasure. For by God's body, Master More – *Indignatio Principis mors est*' ('the wrath of the King is death'). 'Is that all my lord' quoth he. 'Then in good faith is there no more difference between your Grace and me, but that I shall die today and you tomorrow.' And even his old jester, Henry Patenson, proved a Jack Point who kept well clear of the Tower, for he too had sworn the oath.

The Royal Supremacy

At the end of 1534 the Parliament passed an Act of Supremacy, a Second Act of Succession, and an Act of Treasons. In the light of the unqualified assertion of the Royal Supremacy, the new definition of treason is important:

> that if any person or persons . . . do maliciously wish, will or desire by words or writing or by craft imagine, invent practise or attempt any bodily harm to be done to the king's most royal person, the queen's or their heirs apparent, or to deprive them or any of them of their title, dignity or name of their royal estates, or slanderously and maliciously publish and pronounce, by express writing or words that the king our sovereign lord should be a heretic . . .

Cromwell now visited More in the Tower, and reminded him that he was still the King's subject even in prison. More turned away, perhaps brusquely, with a remark which was to be included in the eventual indictment against him –

> I had fully determined with myself neither to study or meddle with any matter of this world but that my whole study should be upon the Passion of Christ, and mine own passage out of this world.

It may be that this was the plain, almost inadvertent word from More which led to the straitening of his conditions, for now all books and writing materials were taken away from him, he was forbidden to receive visitors or to attend Mass.

Fisher was also in the Tower, old and ill, and cold (in a dark hole in Belgium, William Tyndale also shivered, working at Hebrew until the daylight faded and the dark unlit night began). At Christmastide Fisher wrote a pathetic letter to Cromwell, which it must have cost something to write, piteously imploring some better treatment –

I have no more shirts or clothes . . . only frightful rags. I wouldn't mind so much if they kept out the cold. God knows on what thin diet I am constrained to live – at my age my stomach can only take a little food, but if I am deprived of that I fall down from weakness . . .

The letter ends terribly by wishing Cromwell 'a merry Christmas' which might have spoiled a less tough skinned man's Christmas cheer. But it may be

An example of More's Latin handwriting, from the manuscript of his *Expositio Passionis* re-discovered in Spain in 1963.

Thomas More

that this appeal had some effect, for in the next months More's rich Italian friend Bonvisi was able to send More clothing, meat and drink.

The few letters More was able to write in this last period of his imprisonment, deserve their place in any anthology of great Christian literature. What More meant to his children has never been put more beautifully than in one of Margaret's letters to him:

Father, what think you hath been our comfort since your departing from us? Surely the experience we have had of your life past and godly conversation and wholesome counsel and virtuous example and a suretie not only of the continuance of the same, but also a great increase by the goodness of our Lord to the great rest and gladness of your heart devoid of all earthy dregs and garnished with the noble vesture of heavenly virtues, a pleasant palace for the Holy Spirit of God to rest in, who defend you (as I doubt not, good father but of his goodness he will) from all trouble of mind and body and give me your most loving obedient daughter and handmaid and all us your children and friends, to follow that we praise in you.

Robert Bolt's fine drama, *A Man For All Seasons* is after all, a play, and has to contrast 'goodies' and 'baddies', but it does not seem right to make Cromwell the villain of this piece; he was after all, to stand godfather to More's grandson, Thomas the Second, in 1538, which would have been inconceivable, had the family thought him the great enemy.

Fisher was in a different situation from Thomas More. He had defended the Queen in speech and writing. He had boldly attacked those who wished to despoil the Church of her authority and of her goods. He had been compromised with Elizabeth Barton. He had invited Chapuys to appeal to Charles to invade England – treason in any land in any century. He was one of the first to be caught in a crisis of conscience which would lead Catholics to be tried and executed as traitors.

The Silences of Thomas More

More's attitude and his defence were along quite different lines, but no less courageous. One is inevitably reminded of a great Church struggle of our own day, and of Dietrich Bonhoeffer who like Fisher believed in taking arms against a sea of troubles. But More is rather like that noble figure, Helmuth James Count von Moltke, descendant of Field Marshals, but himself opposed to violence, and who refused to take part in the bomb plot to remove a tyrant. Like Thomas More, von Moltke was a lawyer and both men used their love of the law, and their skill in it, to save their lives, and both used to immense effect the weapon of silence. At his trial von Moltke denied the right of his judges to sentence him for his silence, for he had 'only thought'. But at the end, the judge scrawled across the papers – 'He did more than think'.

So Thomas More elected to remain silent. The letters he did not write; the conversations he abruptly ended: the letters he refused to read: the questions he would not answer: the statements he would not pen: the oath he would not swear. He used these weapons skilfully. But they did not save him, for he too, as his accusers knew, did 'more than think'.

His silence exposed tyranny more powerfully than any speech could have done. It all came down in the end to that ultimate privacy of conscience:

'In my conscience' said More 'this was one of the cases in which I was bounden that I should not obey my prince . . . in my conscience the truth seemed to be on the other side . . . wherein I had not informed my conscience neither suddenly or lightly but by long leisure and diligent search for the matter. I leave everyman in his conscience and methinketh that in good faith so were it good conscience every man should leave me to mine.

When they came to take away More's books, Sir Richard Rich was among those present, and he succeeded in entangling More in argument, putting cases in a hypothetical way, and wringing from More, according to Rich, a statement which Cromwell perceived might be used in evidence against him. More by now was quite resigned:

I do nobody harm, I say none harm, but wish everybody good. And if this be not enough to keep a man alive, in good faith I long not to live. And I am dying already . . . and have since I came here been divers times in the case that I thought to die within the hour . . . and therefore my poor body is at the King's pleasure: would God my death would do him good.

When Cromwell next came to the Tower on 3 June 1535 there had been a new happening. Pope Paul III had declared Fisher a Cardinal and the furious authorities sought to find out if it had been in any way solicited or influenced from the English end. It had been discovered that in fact Fisher and More had been able to exchange a few letters and simple gifts. Those letters, against More's wishes, had been burned, so that the prosecution could suggest what they liked about their hypothetical treason, despite More's assertion that they had been commonplace, friendly words.

When in separate interviews, both Fisher and More described the new Act as a 'two edged sword' this was pounced on as proof of collaboration, and therefore of conspiracy.

Now, the Carthusians were to suffer. Roper tells how More was with Meg,

looking out of the window when they had been brought to the Tower, and that
he said 'Look Meg, dost thou not see that these blessed Fathers be now going as
cheerfully to their deaths as Bridegrooms to their marriages?' They died on
19 June, and Fisher was executed on the 22nd. There was a quite different
indictment for More who appeared at Westminster on 1 July to answer a four-
fold charge: that on 7 May 1535 he had remained obstinately and maliciously
silent: that he had corresponded and abetted John Fisher: that their common
assertion that the statute is 'like a two edged sword' proved the charge of aiding
and abetting treason: and that More had declared to Sir Richard Rich that the
King could not be supreme Head of the Church.

Trial

More needed first to defend himself against two charges: one of malice –
and the other that his silence was a 'sure token and demonstration of a corrupt
and perverse nature'.

More replied that 'Of malice, I never spoke anything against it and whatsoever
I have spoken in that matter, I have none otherwise spoken but according to my
very mind, opinion and conscience' – while 'for this my taciturnity and silence
neither your law nor any law in the world is able justly and rightly to punish me,
unless you may besides lay to my charge either some word or some fact in deed'.

He next exposed the weaknesses in the other charges. In respect of the fourth,
it was his word against Richard Rich and he solemnly accused Rich of perjury,
and in a few words discredited the witness, tearing Rich's character to sorry
ribbons. The two other witnesses who had been in the Tower on that occasion,
Richard Southwell and Cromwell's servant Palmer, to their everlasting credit,
said they had been so busy packing up books that they had not listened to the
conversation. It is just possible that there was a misunderstanding, for the
tattered memo of the conversation is unreadable at the critical point. At any
rate the Lord Chancellor was taken aback, and forgot to ask the prisoner
whether he had anything to say before sentence was passed. It was now that
More could speak his mind:

Seeing that I see ye are determined to condemn me (God knoweth how) I
will now in discharge of my conscience speak my mind plainly and freely
touching my indictment and your Statute withal . . .

And forasmuch as this indictment is grounded upon an Act of Parliament
directly repugnant to the laws of God and his holy Church, the supreme
government of which, or any part whereof, may no temporal prince presume

by any law to take upon him, as rightfully belonging to the See of Rome, a spiritual pre-eminence by the mouth of our Saviour himself, personally present on earth, only to St Peter and his successors, Bishops of the same see, by special prerogative granted: it is therefore in law, amongst Christian men, insufficient to charge any Christian man.

He further declared that

this Realm being but one member and small part of the Church might not make a particular law disagreeable with the general law of Christ's Church . . . no more might this realm of England refuse obedience to the See of Rome than a child might refuse obedience to his own natural father.

When Audley reminded him of the determination of the Universities More said:

I am not bounden, my Lord to conform my conscience to the Council of one realm against the general Council of Christendom. For of the foresaid holy bishops I have, for every bishop of yours, one hundred: and for one Council of Parliament (God knoweth what manner of one) I have all the Councils made these thousand years. And for this one kingdom I have all other Christian realms.

When Norfolk retorted 'We now plainly see that ye are maliciously bent', More replied:

Nay, very and pure necessity of my conscience enforceth me to speak so much. Wherein I call and appeal to God whose only sight pierceth into the very depth of man's heart to be my witness.

There may be things touched up in the above statements and we cannot be sure they are More's words. But there is the ring of truth in his final rejoinder:

Howbeit it is not for this Supremacy so much that ye seek my blood, as for that I would not condescend to the marriage.

A Place of Execution

More was declared guilty of high treason, which in that age carried a hideous penalty. The condemned man would be hanged, to the point of near unconsciousness then cut down, disembowelled and his members burned before his eyes. In More's case the sentence was commuted to beheading.

Sir William Kingston, Constable of the Tower, brought More back from Westminster and said farewell 'the tears running down his cheeks'. More said 'Good master Kingston, trouble not yourself but be of good cheer: I will pray for you and my good lady, your wife, that we may meet together in heaven where we shall be merry for ever and ever.' John More and Margaret Roper were waiting at the Tower and got through the halberds of the Yeomen of the Guard, John to kneel for his father's blessing: Meg to embrace her father again and again, to which he kept an unmoved countenance, though in a last note he told how deeply moved he had been. It seems that once again, More wanted to wear his best clothes for his death, but was dissuaded and sent a gold angel to his executioner. The King sent a brutal message telling More to keep his speech short.

When, early on a summer morning, 6 July, More was led out, he no longer resembled the Tudor Worthy of Holbein's painting, but rather the picture of a saint by El Greco, emaciated, skull cap on his head, a long beard, carrying in his hand a red cross. There were not many yards to go, and there was not time enough for some of the more picturesque stories of bystanders to have happened. But one would like to accept the account of his last words, given a few days afterwards, in the so called 'Paris News-Letter' with its sublime last words:

He said little before the execution, only that the people there should pray God for him and he would pray for them. Afterwards he exhorted them and earnestly beseeched them to pray God for the King, so that he would give him good counsel, protesting that he died his good servant, but God's first.

Less reliable in details, Will Roper:

Then desired he all the people about him to pray for him and to bear witness that he should now suffer death in and for the faith of the catholic church. Which done, he kneeled down and after his prayers turned to the executioner and with a cheerful countenance spake thus merrily unto him: Pluck up thy spirits man, and be not afraid to do thine office: my neck is somewhat short, therefore take heed thou strikest not awry, for saving of thine honesty: but if thou doest upon my word I will not hereafter cast it in thy teeth. So at one strike of the executioner passed Sir Thomas More out of this world to God.

The bodies of England's traitors beheaded on Tower Hill were generally flung into the ground of the chapel of St Peter ad Vincula, but it may be that the intercession of More's daughters got him a more seemly burial. His head, exposed on London Bridge, was rescued by Meg Roper and taken home to Canterbury where, opposite the Roper house, it was buried in the little church of St Dunstan.

Thomas More was a prisoner of conscience. There are such prisoners today, of many faiths and of none. But conscience itself is a bare fact, and what clothed More's is perhaps best explained by a verse by Martin Luther, done into English by the other sage of Chelsea, Thomas Carlyle:

And though they take our life,
Goods, honour, children, wife
Yet is their profit small
These things shall vanish all
The City of God remaineth.

Thomas More

As More himself wrote in his own obituary notice:

That he may not shudder with fear at the thought of approaching death, but may meet it gladly with longing for Christ, and that he may find death not completely death for himself, but rather the gateway to a happier life, I beg you, kind reader, attend him with your prayers while he still lives, and also when he has done with life.

FURTHER READING

WORKS

Utopia, trans. by Paul Turner; Penguin Books,
   New York and London.
*A History of King Richard III and Selections from the English
   and Latin Poems*, ed. Richard Sylvester; Yale University Press,
   New Haven and London.
A Dialogue of Comfort Against Tribulation, ed. Frank Manley;
   Yale University Press, New Haven and London.
Selected Letters of Sir Thomas More, ed. E. F. Rogers;
   Yale University Press, New Haven and London.

BIOGRAPHICAL STUDIES

Thomas More, by R. W. Chambers; Jonathan Cape, London and the
   University of Michigan Press, Ann Arbor.
Just Men, by Gordon Rupp; Epworth Press, London.
Lives of Saint Thomas More, by W. Roper and N. Harpsfield;
   Dent, London.
Thomas More and Erasmus, by E. E. Reynolds; Burnes and Oates,
   London and Fordham University Press, New York.
The Field is Won: the Life and Death of Saint Thomas More,
   by E. E. Reynolds; Search Press, London.
Thomas More and Tudor Polemics, by Rainier Pineas;
   Indiana University Press, Bloomington and London.
Thomas More, by James McConica; HMSO, London.